Crosscurrents / MODERN CRITIQUES

Harry T. Moore, *General Editor*

The Angry Young Men
of the Thirties

Elton Edward Smith

WITH A PREFACE BY
Harry T. Moore

SOUTHERN ILLINOIS UNIVERSITY PRESS
Carbondale and Edwardsville

FEFFER & SIMONS, INC.
London and Amsterdam

To our children
Elton and Mary
Esther and Wayne
Stephen and Christine

Library of Congress Cataloging in Publication Data

Smith, Elton Edward, 1915–
    The angry young men of the thirties.

    (Crosscurrents/modern critiques)
    Bibliography: p.
    Includes index.
    1. English poetry—20th century—History and criticism.   I. Title.
PR610.S57   1975   821'.9'1209   74–20731
ISBN 0–8093–0698–0

Contents

Preface

To be alive in the thirties of our century (hardly a "dawn") was not always "bliss," and being young was not always "very Heaven," but many young people of the time wrote of its bad and good sides. Among the English poets of that era, four are generally grouped together because they came along at about the same moment and at times had somewhat similar points of view: C. Day-Lewis, Louis MacNeice, W. H. Auden, and Stephen Spender. The last of them is the youngest, and the only one still alive.

Auden, who has at this time the highest reputation among the quartet, is treated last in the present book, which gives us a full and up-to-date account of these poets and their work. Professor Smith in his final section places these writers historically, seeing them in the perspective of the Romantic writers after the French Revolution and of those "Angry Young Men" of England's 1950s.

Dr. Smith is a seasoned commentator on literature, and his previous books, such as that on William Godwin of the Romantic period (written in collaboration) and the one on Tennyson, a representative Victorian, have deepened his approach to the writers of this century. Further, in 1970, he wrote a volume about one of the poets he now reconsiders in the present book, Louis MacNeice.

In this study, Professor Smith not only shows how thoroughly he is acquainted with his British subject-matter, but also how comprehensively he can write of the Auden-Spender group, dealing with their ideas as well as their modes of expression. He understands these men as they were in the decade of their first fame, and he neatly discusses their significance in the light of this later epoch. His book is informative and skillful, an important contribution in the field of modern literary investigations.

HARRY T. MOORE

Southern Illinois University
September 21, 1974

NOTE: One bit of spelling in this volume needs a word of explanation: we have throughout used a hyphen in the "last name" of Cecil Day-Lewis; he was always listed this way in the British Who's Who.

Introduction

After the publication of a book on Louis MacNeice in 1970, I could go off lightheartedly to a Fulbright-Hays lectureship at the University of Algiers, having attempted to rescue the Anglo-Irish poet from the broad shadow of W. H. Auden and individuality-blunting membership in the Pylon Poets, the Proletarian Poets, the Auden Group.

But in my bag I carried a contract from Southern Illinois University Press to undo all I had done—to restore MacNeice to the milieu from which I had painstakingly separated him. Three historic parallels struck my imagination: the enthusiasm of the British Romantic poets for the French Revolution, the enthusiasm of the proletarian poets for the Marxist revolution, and the enthusiasm for absolutely nothing of their heirs—the Angry Young Men of the fifties.

The only way all these eras and individuals could be worked into one small volume was to limit the time span. So we chose 1930–40 because it was a characteristic decade for all four poets and because it was an important decade in the intellectual history of Western man. A contemporary poet, William Harmon, returned from Vietnam as Navy commander, claimed that he could still smell the "odor of the Thirties" in London, a decade which he describes as the time when curly liberals first "thought it out," then went to Spain and "fought it out," and perhaps in the process got their "earnest brains blown out."

At the Bodleian Library, after a long talk with Dr. E. R.

Dodds, Regius Professor of Greek at Oxford and Louis MacNeice's literary executor, first editions of all four poets, a desk, a key, a quiet room and my noisy American typewriter combined to produce this study. In its conclusion I attempt, albeit sketchily, to indicate the direction each poetic career took after the 1930s.

I am most grateful to the Bodleian, to my own University Library, to William H. Taft and the Sponsored Research Council for grants from the University of South Florida which made possible the collation of notes that developed into this book, to my esteemed colleague, H. Christian Kiefer, for its title, and to my chairman, John R. Clark, for encouragement and aid.

Grateful acknowledgment is extended for quotations from the following works of C. Day-Lewis: "Transitional Poem," "Johnny Head-In-Air," and "Letter to W. H. Auden," from *Collected Poems of C. Day Lewis* (London: Jonathan Cape, with the Hogarth Press, 1954), copyright by C. Day-Lewis, reproduced by permission of the Executors of the Estate of C. Day-Lewis and Jonathan Cape, Ltd., and the Hogarth Press; also reprinted by permission of The Harold Matson Co., Inc. Quotations reprinted from *Starting Point* (London: Jonathan Cape, 1937; New York: Harper & Brothers, 1938) by permission of A. D. Peters & Co., and The Harold Matson Co., Inc.

Grateful acknowledgment is extended for quotations from the following works of Stephen Spender: *World Within World: Autobiography* (London: Hamish Hamilton, 1951; New York: Harcourt, Brace and Company, 1951), copyright by Stephen Spender, reprinted by permission of The Harold Matson Co., Inc., and by permission of A. D. Peters & Co. *The Backward Son: A Novel* (London: Hogarth Press, 1940), reprinted by permission of The Hogarth Press, Ltd. "The Dead Island," "The Cousins," and "The Burning Cactus," from *The Burning Cactus* (London: Faber and Faber, 1936; New York: Random House, 1936) reprinted by permission of Faber and Faber, Ltd., and Random House.

The Destructive Element: A Study of Modern Writers and Beliefs (London: Jonathan Cape, 1935; Philadelphia: Albert Saifer, 1953), reprinted by permission of Jonathan Cape, Ltd., and The Harold Matson Co., Inc. *The New Realism: A Discussion* (London: Hogarth Press, 1939), reprinted by permission of The Hogarth Press, Ltd.

Grateful acknowledgment is extended for permission to quote from "Bagpipe Music" from *The Collected Poems of Louis MacNeice*, edited by E. R. Dodds, copyright © The estate of Louis MacNeice 1966 (New York: Oxford University Press, 1967). Quotations reprinted by permission of the Oxford University Press and Faber and Faber, Ltd., the British publisher.

ELTON SMITH

University of South Florida
Tampa
June 1974

The Angry Young Men of the Thirties

C. Day-Lewis: The Iron Lyricist

The ten years from 1930 to 1940 had all the headlong pace of a wave rising out of the deep trough of World War I, pushing upward with remarkable passion and idealism, curling over, hesitating, then crashing down thunderously into the disaster of World War II. The dominant figure of the preceding epoch, Woodrow Wilson, had sounded a note of peaceful promise: "We shall prevail . . . as sure as . . . God reigns!"

Whether they believed God reigned or not, it was a heady time of passionate idealism for young Englishmen of left-wing persuasion. The pacifism of the Oxford Peace Pledge, the expansive sympathies of Leon Blum's Popular Front, milk for bomb-orphans in Spain, clothing for displaced Basques, and illuminating all social endeavors, the bright morning light from the Communist dynamo in Russia. But Wilson could thunder the denunciation of a prophet of doom as well as trill the promise of the dove of peace: "I have seen fools resist Providence before, and I have seen their destruction—as will come . . . again—utter destruction and contempt." [1]

As often happens, we still await the promise of the dove; but the prophecy of doom was promptly and efficiently fulfilled. Stocks crashed on Wall Street in 1929. Three and one-half million unemployed in England, seven million in Germany, sixteen million in the United States. A period of "depressed areas," crowded with "Threadbare Common Men" standing idle under lampposts at street corners.

Auden and his friends lived an inner roseate life of high hope in an outer world grey and squalid, "smokeless chimneys, damaged bridges, rotting wharves and choked canals." If Wilson stood at the beginning, a spare, puritan figure of hope and warning, the period ended in a thunderous Wagnerian *Götterdämmerung*, whose Corporal hero was immolated along with the world he had destroyed.

C. Day-Lewis delineated the problem faced by all of the poets of so fragmented and divided an era. How can a poet write, in the year 1934 (A *Hope for Poetry*) [2] without a homogeneous audience, born in a unified culture, able to catch allusions, recognize myths, and share experience? W. H. Auden has shown two ways a poet may react: he may take the private emblems and language of a small, fashionable ingroup and attempt to extend them in the comprehension of the larger public, or he may salvage those elements of a disintegrating culture that are still shared and alive and use them to communicate with his world (cf. T. S. Eliot). Auden not only pointed out these ways, he exemplified both.

But Day-Lewis himself, when compared with Auden, was "a talent less self-willed, less boisterous, less robust; a talent which left to itself, might even have kept aloof from politics." [3] When Dilys Powell made this comparison, she had before her five volumes of Day-Lewis's poetry, of which three were clearly nonpolitical in nature, one fell between categories, and the fifth was political. The observation Powell made in 1934 has remained relevant since most of Day-Lewis's work after the 1930s has been nonpolitical in nature. However, Day-Lewis himself offers a warning lest we should leap to hasty conclusions: "if you go through the work of contemporary poets—even the comparatively few who are known as 'political'—you will be surprised to find what a small proportion of their poems deal with political subjects." [4] Thus, in the works of C. Day-Lewis in the decade 1930–40, we meet a poet who in volume says perhaps the least of any of the group about politics, but who in quality of dedication, within that least, says perhaps the most explicit things.

Day-Lewis's first volume, *Beechen Vigil* (1925), was more closely related to the Romantic past or the Georgian present, than to the future of England. The very title of *Country Comets*, his next publication, in 1928, disqualifies it as a serious attempt to awaken a sleeping world. The title is taken from Andrew Marvell: "Ye country comets, that portend / No war nor prince's funeral, / Shining unto no higher end / Than to presage the grass's fall." J. Alfred Prufrock, vacationing in the country, might have insisted that he had not come to play Hamlet, nor even to swell the progress of a company of local lords, but only to watch the cutting of the grass! "To Her Whose Mind and Body are a Poetry I have Not Achieved, I Give These Poems" is the handsome dedication. The poems achieve special unity because they are "all direct products of a single conflict whose recurrence I could neither expect nor desire" (Foreword, p. vii). The conflict (more specifically stated in *Transitional Poem*) is between competing philosophic answers to the question of life's perennial choices between the specific and the general: abstract beauty or the loveliness of a particular maiden, a predetermined universe in which man is a mindless monad or a planless universe in which man is a free nomad? This same tension will emerge in his novel of 1938, *Starting Point*, as "contradictions" at one point and as "opposites" at another.

Despite the disclaimer of the epigraph, *Country Comets* introduces many of the philosophic themes to be developed more fully in *Transitional Poem*, sounded in *From Feather to Iron* and echoed in *The Magnetic Mountain*, get shouted down in the violent *A Time to Dance* and *Overtures to Death*, and finally die away in *Word Over All*. In "Prelude" the theatrical conjurer will rehearse his skill to make the audience remember dreams which were unfulfilled. He will use for his stage properties the beauty of a young girl who did not give her love. The word *untrue* introduces a perennial conflict in the poet's mind concerning the nature of reality: rational and absolute, or particular and fleeting? As Shelley shrieked and fell under the overwhelming passion of his call to poetry, so Day-Lewis hears a voice in "Sun and

Waterfall" crying across the valley where everything is perishing and slipping into the past, asking who will keep the whole framework of life from sinking into dissolution? The poet falls to the earth; the call provides no motive power by its vision: the vast inertia of nature and humanity simply claims one more martyr. But his rising hope is that some few ears may hear the "trumpet call" above the petty affairs of men's little lives.

"Cyprian! Cyprian!" celebrates the only thing that is real —the particular beauty of sunlight shining off one woman's eyes. Reason, philosophy, and poetry alike fade before her touch, her voice, and her body. Thus, as a natural development from "Cyprian! Cyprian!" "Naked Woman with Kotyle" reverses Keats's Grecian urn. Instead of art making life both beautiful and immortal, the artist's vase is too petty and frail to capture all her living beauty.

"It Is the True Star" is by far the most philosophical poem in the total collection, with an argument that moves in four logical steps. First, is a man's life only a dream-role which he plays in a theater where he is both actor and audience? Albert Camus, in *Sisyphus*, might answer affirmatively: yes, there is no essential difference between the historical Julius Caesar and the actor who plays his part each night in the revival of Shakespeare's play. But this is not Day-Lewis's answer. He cannot accept the well-known distinction between being and nonbeing of Jean-Paul Sartre. Instead he insists, in the second place, that all man's projections of his inner dreams must be tested by the touchstone of the " 'perhaps' " of the objective world. And at this point he seems to be preparing for at least partial acceptance of some such materialistic philosophy as communism. In a brilliant wordplay, he asks if man is monad or nomad. As monad he is part of a full-fledged system but he has lost freedom; as nomad he has so much freedom that he has lost all relationship to a coherent system. Day-Lewis shouts a resounding "No" to both of these choices, and, reflecting that Leibnitz had once said that a monad had no windows, throws his own window open, sticks out his head, and discovers that the star which guides his life is one he himself flings out into whatever skies he chooses—and so joins Camus after all! But by his references to Columbus and Napoleon, Day-Lewis seems to insist that the projection must have enough coherence with material, external reality that the personal gesture achieves a high level of success. Then he joins Samuel Taylor Coleridge in projectionism by claiming that although nature is really there, it is we who interpret her as sad or glad ("Dejection"). It is this same interpretive power that ranks us with the Creator, sharing the powers of godhead.

"Between Hush and Hush" also prepares the mind of the poet for eventual acceptance of Marxian materialism, as it renounces the hope of any life after death, and leaves man in existential fashion, with the *angst* of a human perfection which lasts for only a single "blink" of time. "Under the Willow" makes a fleeting identification of the opposing poles of mind and matter that Day-Lewis was perpetually trying to mate. In stanza 2, the poet considers triumphantly that the lovers have found a microscope which has the power to unite mind and matter in the tiny moment of bliss even though they may have found no telescope with which to unite the great macrocosm outside.

"Wreck Near Ballinacarig" joins "Between Hush and Hush" in the denial of god. When the bereft lover looks at an old wrecked vessel on the beach, he is sure that when it smashed up, no God heeded. "The Perverse" plays the game of absolute versus particular until the head spins. Being denied love, he sulks with the absolute awhile. Love being offered, he has to translate bare breasts into "thin philosophies." Love being gone, he dreams of warm, loving fulfillment at night. When he is finally fulfilled, he cannot wait, like Pygmalion, to turn his lover's body into the stone of thought. So in this seesaw poem which comes just before the final Apologue, one senses that the merging of absolute and particular which the poet celebrated in "It Is the True Star" and "Under the Willow, II" is neither so certain nor so lasting as his temporary trumpet tones suggested.

Transitional Poem (1929) continues the same search for order, but as its title suggests, the search is merely on its way to something at which it has not arrived and therefore it is unfair to view it as a finished and coherent philosophic statement. Thus when David Daiches [5] states that the conflicts of the poem remain unresolved, due to the poet's habit of alternating poems expressing conflicting points of view, he is only agreeing with the poet's own estimate. Because it is transitional, it is bound to be ambiguous, with a goal which is as yet partly unidentified and completely unattained. In a letter to Raymond Tschumi, Day-Lewis explained: " 'My method in the first three volumes was to move round an experience in a sequence of poems, approaching it thus at a number of different angles, and trying to discover . . . what truth lay beneath.' " [6]

Part 1 begins with a quotation from Maximian, who, on a journey, was seduced by a Greek courtesan and reduced to temporary impotence: "Ira brevis, longa est pietas, recidiva voluptas; Et cum posse perit, mens tamen una manet." (Passion is short, loyalty is lasting, sexual joy returns; when the physical possibility perishes, only one's attitude of mind remains.) [7] The schoolboy looks at the world and sees disorder everywhere. His well-trained mind tells him that until the phenomena of life have the "symmetry of brain" stamped upon them, there will be no way for man to understand and possess life. He can joke about the cosmic predicament of a mere mortal trying to wrest faith from the eternal flux. Then, establishing a criterion which really makes its attainment impossible, he insists with schoolboy shrillness that the mind must be capable of coping with everything or nothing, a dichotomy which almost answers that in such case it can cope with nothing. Lolling on Lillington Common (part 1, stanza 3), the poet feels so complacent that he is tempted to accept the unthinking premises of Tom, Dick, and Harry. Even when he builds a fire and feels like a little section of plateau sloping off into the darkness of annihilation on both sides, yet he recalls that he was the maker of the fire and therefore of cosmic importance. Perhaps if only he could be content with alternation between opposites: lover of flesh today, tomorrow lover of spirit, now finite, now infinite, he would be saved the profound labor of non-attainment and the quest for a Grail never reached. The classic form of the total poem as well as the intellectual dilemma is dualistic, "twin poles" (stanza 4) which in their profound attraction and repulsion crackle with electrical energy. Both are constant, but each is unsatisfying alone. The poet, "Dismayed by the monstrous credibility / Of all antinomies" (stanza 6), seeks answers to his paradoxes by returning to the scenes of his youth. At least the earth demands no rational structure: it can point up its arguments just as well with a sick sheep as a primrose. But this does not help the poet who is under a compulsion to make some statement of order. The illusion of order can come only from abstraction. Yet in stanza 7 the poet scorns abstraction, maintaining that if Homer had no experience with actual women, the epic form would have been buried forever beneath his blindness.

Part 2 begins with a most appropriate epigraph from Walt Whitman's *Leaves of Grass*: "Do I contradict myself: / Very well, then, I contradict myself." In January, 1929, Day-Lewis made his own explanation of *Transitional Poem* and then buried it in the notes at the end of the volume. The central theme was to be the single mind. The poem would be divided into four parts, representing four phases of a man's personal experiences on the way to single-mindedness. "It will be seen that a transition is intended from one part to the next such as implies a certain spiritual progress and a consequent shifting of aspect." These aspects may be termed: (1) metaphysical, (2) ethical, (3) psychological; while (4) is an attempt to relate the poetic impulse with the totality of man's experience. "Formally the parts fall with fair accuracy into the divisions of a theorem in geometry, *i.e.* general enunciation, particular enunciation, proof, corollaries." Thus the first part was to be metaphysical, or in terms of a geometric theorem, general enunciation—a metaphor to be expected of poets who liked to suggest scientific objectivity and logical impeccability in a field usually considered to be impervious to such considerations.

Part 2 was to be ethical experience or the enunciation of a particular phase of life. It is time, says the poet, to declare his allegiances, and he proceeds to list a group of friends:

his beloved, a hawk-faced man who could call an apple a peach and still win the argument, " 'a brazen leech,' " and a "tow-haired poet" (perhaps Auden? [stanza 8]) who was always working away at some gnomic prop to hold up his all-too-stable universe; steady in conduct as an old horse, his mind was quick and darting. As his single mind coped with the split intelligence of Day-Lewis, he produced a piebald mixture of truth and nonsense.

Once the poet desired fame, but Ulysses and Herodotus, who were simply after land, goods, or women, got glory thrown in. He might become a teacher, learn to discipline his too-large desire for heroic quest and philosophical Hesperides, and settle into the contentment of the English countryside. But he cannot bear to settle down, and considers this to be just another specious resolution of his dilemma, because he is not a vegetable to put down roots, nor an animal to wander about mindlessly. If a man lets himself sink into the seasonality of nature, he denies his capacity to project his special star into the heavens. Somewhere between the two extremes of surrender to nature and rejection of nature lies the limited empiricism the poet chooses: to accept nature as the raw material for the artist and as the groundwork of man's natural existence, but to affirm that man has infinite potential for its exploration and control. A very brief poem of four quatrains (stanza 13), only two feet to the line, dismisses the usual solutions: commonsense acceptance of mystery (a mole counting stars), sex, or religion. But the poet is not a mole to burrow (he makes no comment on the alternative of sex!) nor a mantis to pray, but a man who sees stars and defines them by the gaps between. This is perhaps as far as Day-Lewis ever gets in terms of solutions, and it is notable that while each statement of antithesis is clear and sharp, each statement of solution is vague and metaphorical. But in stanza 14 Day-Lewis refuses to accept the idea of continuing tensions, both of which must have their due, and claims that we have to seize one horn or the other in any antithesis. So we watch a natural-born dualist struggling vainly to become a monist.

Part 3 employs an epigraph from Herman Melville: "But even so, amid the tornadoed Atlantic of my being, do I myself still centrally disport in mute calm." It is hard to understand in what sense part 3 can be considered either "psychological" or "proof," so much so that the comment of the notes sounds a little bit like intellectual swank imported after the poems were written. The section does defend the dilemma of the poet. Anybody who scorns the problem he is raising has lived only amidst the unreal ("unicorns"). If one has never pursued an argument and discovered that the way to reach the west is to go due east, he has never really thought. But choosing and rejecting neither, he turns toward the true north and finds it magnetic to his desire (cf. "magnetic continent," stanza 23, part 4, and the later work *The Magnetic Mountain*). There will he find the icy, glacierlike authority he seeks.

Part 3 of *Transitional Poem*, stanza 19, reviews the stages through which the poet has already passed. At first he was the youth insistent upon an intellectual framework for the world and disdainful of everything but passionless perfection. Even in the sunshine Achilles kept on his overcoat. But now older, the poet swings to the opposite extreme and will concentrate on bodies, until he discovers that they too deflect the sunshine. Love places man in a twosome; the resulting pregnancy makes man part of a threesome which in turn is part of all the world. Still seeking something higher (stanza 20), he rejects any Platonic distillation of real and actual, but the old longing remains for some successful fusion of body and mind. As he thinks of the coming child, he recognizes that beginnings are totally unrelated to ideas of cosmic purpose or personal immortality. Nevertheless that instinctual life must be given disciplined control, even if it is only the loop-line of a railway, on which the engine, quite satisfied, always travels the same way and returns to the same point. Stanza 21 completes the transformation of early love (a "meteor") into a domestic habitual round (the "loop-line"). Even the death of flowers (early love) enriches the total earth.

Stanza 24 retraces the same pattern of development: the

"cold storage" of youthful reason breaks out into extreme sexuality, followed by the demand for a single mind which will fuse the two extremes of cold and hot. Such singleness of mind (stanza 25) is not to be found in unreal flights of the deductive mind in the thin, higher air, nor in molish dark tunneling in the earth below, but in some kind of creative acceptance of diversity. The section closes with an interesting denial that real fusion is possible; the dream and the act always remain apart in this perfectionless earth.

Part 4 turns to a contemporary and friend—W. H. Auden —for another fine epigraph with sharply distinct antinomies of night and day, spirit and beast. But actually Day-Lewis's poem is based on the first verses of the Gospel According to John. "In the beginning was the Word [infancy]; And the Word was with God [childhood]; And the Word was God [early youth]; And the Word was made flesh [expulsion into maturity]." It is a good thing to have been thrown out of Eden, otherwise every prophecy of man would only be an echo of that great voice. So mankind assaults the cliffs of the absolute (the sword-guarded eastern gate of the Garden of Eden), falls back, but keeps returning to a persistent attrition (stanzas 28, 29).

When he knew beauty in a particular girl, she became poetry. Now he realizes that the projectionism of the mind is such that beauty is, by some dark caprice which he himself does not understand, directed outward, or confined inward. His state when first in love was like an electric light bulb, painful, dancing upon a point of wire, batteries of electric current passing into a small globe of frosted glass. Now since he has broken free of the antinomies, the globe breaks, light and power are both alike set free. Now he can take a telescope to see stars and a microscope to enlarge a flea, or let the summer sun pass through it as a "burning-glass" (stanza 32) to make experience more intense, and to force the meaning of his lines to leap into flame. Once he used to string lanterns of poetry between the horns of dilemmas, thus vainly hoping to draw them together. Now he tunes in a cosmic radio from which he draws hints, omens, and ambiguities concerning the central meaning of the earth.

Stanza 33 gives hints of social criticism, with its reference to the rusting ironworks of abandoned mines, the betrayal of human owners by the earth, and the prophetic promise that there are going to be great changes made in the world in this very era. The hawk has seen the blank contours of the earth from on high. Now he simply wheels in contemplation. The lark which ascended the dawn sky and flooded heaven with song descends at nightfall to his favorite tree. And so the poet—hawk to give sharpest scrutiny to his world, and lark to flood the earth with song— may now rest in peace, night, and quietness.

In *Transitional Poem* Day-Lewis worked out the major premises of a philosophic position which could be further explored or expanded but not basically changed. Man does not live in a rational universe which forces its framework upon him; there is no God who determines his existence or conduct; the mind alone is powerless to include all earth's infinite variety. Not immortal, man's life on earth is all he has, but—and this is the crucial part of the argument—man may fashion his world as he will and thus take upon himself some of the character of godhead.

Although Day-Lewis's solution may get him off the hook of antinomies, it certainly leaves him hung up on the challenge of social responsibility. If God makes the world the way it is, He is responsible. If man is simply an animal part of nature, nature is responsible. But if man is capable of shaping his world, then man is responsible. This is a responsibility which will be explored at the level of a husband and wife during the period of gestation of a child in *From Feathers to Iron*. Its social aspects will be linked with the vast pilgrim band of *The Magnetic Mountain*. It will become the challenge behind the warning cries of impending doom to be found in *A Time to Dance* and *Overtures to Death*.

In publishing his next series of related poems, *From Feathers to Iron* (1931), Day-Lewis found himself the victim of an amusing misunderstanding. So firmly had it been embedded in the critics' minds that this was a poet of social significance, that to the lyrical narrative of the nine months of waiting for the birth of their first child, the critics attached all sorts of symbolic political meanings (A *Hope for Poetry*, chapter 6). Yet, despite the poet's disclaimers, there are at least political overtones to this highly personal poem dedicated "To the Mother." The epigraphs and title are taken from W. H. Auden's meditation that thoughts may grow out to feathery dead ends and from the writings of John Keats: "We take but three steps from feathers to iron."

Day-Lewis adds his interpretation to what Auden and Keats had to say about feathers and iron, when he compares the days of courtship and lovers' wings flying lightly over time and space with the present period of pregnancy when the wings must be folded and become sterner, harder stuff—iron, for example. Although the poetic image is striking and the lyric narrative personal, there is a kind of social commentary in the relationship of a man and a woman, having passed through the carefree hedonism of courtship, and having taken in the hushed silence the awesome vows of matrimony, who now find that they must prepare for parenthood.

So this new autumn wind whirls the summer leaves and easy ways away together. They must move from interpersonal experiment to what the poet calls, with some economic suggestion, the "trade routes" (poem 4) more commonly traveled. Now no more flitting, only the steady pilgrimage toward a shared and desired goal. This is no longer a "pleasure" trip; they are now carrying freight. No longer do they whirl through the empyrean in careless ecstasy; they are serving the state in the making of a new citizen; they are enlarging the population of the world by one. Together they are building a strong ship to sail for a new continent. The sensual approach wanes; they concentrate on the dark room of the womb where the negative and nonliving will become the positive and living. Somehow an end is suggested in this beginning—another dark room, this time a tomb, where positives return to negatives. At birth we groan in parturition; in death we groan in parting. But as the new seed of their child lies in the older earth of his mother's body, so they will have to seek the

new world by following the old ways—a surprising bit of
conservatism as the poet's political predilections bow to the
inevitable reign of biology.

As Day-Lewis considers his wife's pregnancy he recognizes that there will be some loss to his wife's beauty
(poem 5), but he considers that the gain of the new life
will more than compensate for the loss. As an appropriate
setting for this birth, they leave the town and return to the
countryside. In this and many other ways Day-Lewis reveals himself as the most Georgian of the modern poets
with a mystical identification with earth and all growing
green things. They must now work harder for the support
of this new life; this earthly life in the countryside is self-
sufficient; the maturation of a fetus needs no justification.
Life essentially is linked with heat of body, passion, and
affection: the reasonableness of mind is all later and deriva-
tive.

Then as William Butler Yeats penned a letter to his infant daughter and Louis MacNeice to his unborn child,
Day-Lewis expresses his hopes for his son or daughter
(poem 18). Either let the child be a pioneer, lean and hard,
with coat off, lonely but dedicated. Or let the child be a
clockwork doll who learns to wag in perfect time to the
wag of the world. Or perhaps it is in such new lives that
the world will regain integrity and turn away from the
flatterers, the pimps, the fakes. Will the child be a conformist? Will he even thank his parents and the world for
an inheritance of bankrupt firms, worn-out factory machinery, exhausted farms?

He dares not wish too much for his child; it's a treacherous world at best, but only that instead of treading water
to barely stay afloat, it may get its feet firmly on rock. If
lucky, it may have the outward graces that ease all relationships. The child has a good mother; when he first met her
he knew from his eyes' delight that he need look no further.
Now the acres that were his delight feed another life and he
is sure that the fare is good. All of this rather pleasant
musing is shattered by the panic thought that his wife might
die in childbirth. But the tremor of terror is soon replaced

by the genial invitation of the father to step outside into the sunlight—a man has been born (poem 29).

Clearly arising out of *Transitional Poem, The Magnetic Mountain* continues the metaphor of magnetic attraction, the author's love of metallic reference, and the prophetic call to a great work in the world. It begins with the elements in the old culture that must be abandoned. It moves to the qualifications for the kind of men who may make the pilgrimage. It ends with great crowds upon the road, drawn by the attractive power of the mountain. Unlike *Pilgrim's Progress*, although this is a real pilgrimage which requires the individual preparation of iron souls purified by fire; it never reaches the Heavenly City, perhaps because the road must be built by the pilgrims all the way, and surely because such a goal exceeds the power of the poet to convey; in the area of the miraculous mountain a compass no longer points, clocks no longer tick, space stands on its head, and time doubles back upon itself.

The poem opens with the warning that the goal cannot be achieved on the same ground where the pilgrims stand by some simple change of environment. Thus part 1, dedicated to W. H. Auden, is preceded by an epigraph of social pilgrimage from the writings of Rex Warner, inviting comrades in the spring to set out on a journey which will do good to all the masses of the earth. The couplet is significant because it suggests that the poem issues a general invitation and that all who accept are to be comrades in a new movement. Like the spring, it represents a new beginning, more a matter of heart than of head; it is epic and massive rather than heroic and individual, and it begins to establish the good life among all men. Seldom has an epigraph provided a better outline of the work it was chosen to grace.

The third poem of part 1 states a great deal that in Day-Lewis's usual fashion is either repeated in other poems or shown from another point of view. The magnetic mountain with its marvelous attractive power lies beyond the railheads of the mind and cannot be achieved by reason. It achieves the very thing that rational mind, desire of the heart, and dedication of the spirit have never been able to achieve alone—connecting the airy upper element of sky with the heavy lower weight of earth.

Its access requires true pioneering because no railroad goes so far. There are rusty tracks and rotting ties where other men tried and lost heart—and life. The kestrel (Holy Ghost?), which is usually connected with joy, may hover over that place, but the journey to it will require men with iron in their souls—Day-Lewis's fondness for the movement from feathers to metal, from bird to iron. Their spirits will be blades tempered in fire, and the truth shall show them the way. Once reached, they will find a mine of metal so deep that it shields its workers from all adverse winds. The mineral will form girders to take the sag out of the sky. It is true that there is enough raw material to make an individual explorer rich, but the essential thing is that there is enough metal there to build a cantilever bridge right over the chaos of our time.

In poem 4 the poet dedicates himself to go to the mountain. But before he leaves for the future, he is going to take a light engine back along the tracks to inspect the moribund past. When he sets out, he hopes to catch up with his good friends Wystan (Auden) and Rex (Warner). He will find good friends, a good country, and make a clean sweep of all the past, or come to the clean end of death trying. In a pedestrian prose analysis, it is impossible to suggest the verve and zest of the poem, the marvelous lyric way it swings along, the diction that makes it sound like a large company of men singing, its pace that never seems to flag throughout a work of fifty-five pages.

Part 2, the reexamination of the old world, takes as its epigraph the appropriate words of William Blake: "Drive your cart and your plough over the bones of the dead." This part of the long poem is treated as a court trial in which the old world is represented by four defendants. The first, the poet's mother, calls her son to be natural, to live the common round of life, to reject the intellectual vanity which requires that one step outside the natural order in order to control it. In an interesting echo of Christ's words to his mother when she urged him to perform his first miracle at the marriage feast of Cana—"Woman, . . . my time is not yet come"—the poet calls his mother "woman," and demands that she ask no more of him than he has already given. For her to call him to continued filial duty is to demand an atavistic rite, to prolong her own life by transfusing his young blood into her old veins.

The second defendant seems to represent a public school education. He invokes the famous men of the past and claims that it's a good land, just as it is; why is any pilgrimage necessary? It's wartime and patriotism demands that they work together. Take a sporting chance, play the game, be a man, keep the rules, don't you want to win? The poet-prophet replies that there is need for men to volunteer for all sorts of dangerous duties, but their main job will not be to preserve the old order, but to cut away all the old tangles, to break through all the blockages and stoppages of modern society, to get the living in touch with each other, and to raise the dead. But the men to do it will have to give up playing with toys, they must go into strictest discipline. They will have to forget much of what they have been taught in school. They must be men who sing at work, who can drill hard without special uniforms and insignia.

The third defendant is a clergyman who states his past services to the state and thereby reveals his religious infidelity. An amateur psychologist, he makes gods for men in their own image and at their specific order: dark demons for savages, patriots for Hebrews, comforters for Christians, myths for atheists. The Church has never been a leader and therefore cannot be held responsible for the mess the world is in; it barely hangs on to the skirts of progress or revolution. Compromisingly, it is always ready to order an anodyne to the defeated and to bless the victors. The poet-prophet showers curses on the clergyman, God's "middleman," who domesticates zeal and deals with the soul in the terms of the "petty bourgeois." He brands a Cain for murder of his brother on his way to bless a submarine. But time is past for all that atavistic nonsense, the medicine man must now be forced to take his own medicine.

The fourth defendant pleads for the familiarity of place, the goodness of this earth, and the poet-prophet replies that such sentiments drive a stake deep in the earth but never risk anything by attempting to fly. The poet's own wife steps forward as witness for the fourth defendant. She is another advocate of the natural life of domestic love, one's own table, a familiar landscape. She wants to be a person of consequence, admired by others, but the one who should have been her chief possession refuses to be possessed and keeps looking right through her up to the stars. The poet persists in setting art (the primordial creative act) over chaos (the variety of nature's cyclic changefulness). Stars draw him instead of her eyes. He replies that she must remain just as she is, but in his house, where she is to be completely at home, there will always be one room of dream and purpose that she may not enter.

Part 3's epigraph is from D. H. Lawrence: "Never yield before the barren." It begins with a song in honor of W. H. Auden's departure for America. He is a member of the pilgrim band. Looking west, tired of the old stifling ways, he will fly high alone, bird, aviator, and the poet's friend.

Then the four defendants are replaced by four enemies on a cosmic battlefield. The first enemy, sensuality, is told that this is no time to play amorous games; the hammer is held over us and the sickle has been sharpened and the poet-prophet cannot stay to argue. The second enemy is the journalist who drugs the populace with cheap vicarious thrills, thus keeping them from recognizing the unsatisfactoriness of their lives (a theme of Auden and Isherwood in *The Ascent of F6*). Disdaining to reply to the journalist directly, the poet instead cautions his readers. He tells the men to drop that evening paper, don't they know it's poison? He asks the women if they aren't ashamed to be taking dope? He threatens to reduce editors back into their native element, pulp. The third enemy would seem to be the religion of pseudoscience with its clinical Trinity: Eugenics, Eupeptics, and Euthanasia. In reply, the poet claims that the true god hides himself from the many but sends a clear call to the chosen, who immediately dispose of all of this world's goods so as to be light and free for pilgrimage. The fact that the false views of god are attributed exclusively to scientists recalls D. H. Lawrence rather than Karl Marx. When Day-Lewis asserts that god cannot be determined empirically by the use of a telescope, he is not maintaining that god does not exist, he is only asserting that god cannot be approached scientifically. Day-Lewis, the Marxists, and Lawrence all agreed that intellectual or scientific conceptions of god are false; but only Lawrence would have agreed with Day-Lewis's further contention that there is a god, although to experience him is an emotional rather than an intellectual process. A description of where this god is to be found emphasizes emotional apprehension and the experience of physical nature. Nightingales or poplars, they know him, and man, too, but only in moments of high excitement, or of heightened perception, or of great joy. When men have this experience, god seems to be in their hearts; his presence is very near—a quite orthodox description of the mystic visions of the saints.

The fourth enemy is a dreamer, a poet, a lover of nature—in other words, the poet now sees himself as foe. And his answer is addressed to his own recessive tendency to retreat from a malign environment into a private inner world. But he must face the new condition that no retreats are available any more. The setting for his poetry will no longer be the bank of a stream, but a circle of bayonets; to sing a new song that will sound steely rather than soft.

The Gerard Manley Hopkins epigraph to part 4 continues the admonition to a stern sense of mission: "He comes with work to do, he does not come to coo." In part 4 of *The Magnetic Mountain* the older ways to happiness have been irretrievably lost. The old world that lies behind us is going up in flames. The poet asks where the savior can be, where is there an end to the world's sickness, where is the mountain where they may be healed and their hearts steeled for the pioneer journey still ahead? The answer states that the leader for such a pilgrimage must be one who soars with birds and feeds with sheep—a rather old idea of "head in clouds, feet on earth," but expressed strongly and freshly. Wystan Auden, Rex Warner, and Day-Lewis all claim this

new world as their own. But some will have to be left behind, and there follows an eighteenth-century list of the
humors: Lipcurl, Swiveleye, Bluster, Crock, Queer, Mister
I'll-think-it-over, Miss Not-to-day, Young Who-the-hell-
cares, Old Let-us-pray, Sir Apres-moi-le-deluge.

The journey to the magnetic mountain is not a matter of
distance (poem 28), nor simply of thinking, but of committed position. Having taken that step of commitment to
the new world, a man will discover that the magnet that
draws is himself and the steel that disciplines along the line
of march is also himself. The poet begins to say that the
new world flowers out of the dark, then bethinks himself
of his contemporary idiom and his proletarian alignment
and changes from flowers to tools, dynamos, bridges, towers,
tractors, and cranes—all, of course, notably metallic.

Poem 31 states a utopian hope that is an important part
of early Marxist idealism. After the journey is over and the
iron discipline (dictatorship) is past, and all the world has
become part of the classless society, then there will be hap-
pier times, then the hearts will be whole, then men may
indulge in sports and couples in love. Then the individual
may permit himself solo flights across the sea, or the break-
ing of athletic records; then men may rejoice in landscapes
and the fall of light upon a hill. But this is not yet the
utopia; this is the stern era of a wind that will shake the
world.

Poem 33 returns once more to survey the world to be
left behind. Ironically, it begins with an invitation to survey William Blake's "green and pleasant land." Such a survey will reveal many of his "dark satanic mills." Day-Lewis
names some of the authors of corruption and decay: yes-
men, pansies, politicians, prelates, pressmen, back-slappers,
cheer-leaders, broadcasting announcers who pronounce "All-
Clear" when the enemy squadron is drawing near. Such
men yawn at disaster; is there nothing in which they believe?

The next poem is dedicated to Frances Warner; poems
35 and 36 culminate in a final drinking chorus. On the magnetic mountain a beacon burns to announce world peace,

and all men's eyes turn from it to the sunlight. Let the beacon be lighted soon and let the sun be seen soon! Men must break out of their trance, begin the dance of a comradely life, and turn, all together, toward the light.

Whereas Auden recognized the integral connection between social neurosis and individual illness and seems to have considered that both could be cured by a resolute change of mind, when Day-Lewis takes hold of the same stick, he does so from the opposite end. The central issue is not simply to provide therapy to neurotic individuals and thus to cure the ills of society. Alas, it is not *simply* anything. But somehow individual and society are one, diagnosis and prescription the same. The cure must therefore be one, but just as the poet has had great difficulty fusing mental opposites, so he has great fuzziness in expressing exactly what the social cure may be. The cure, whatever it may be, starts with the group and moves to the individual. Then, after the establishment of world socialism, the individual may once again regain his importance and his idiosyncracies, but such self-indulgent individualism is taboo in the searing survey of society's ills and the exhausting march with its emphasis on the whole rather than the one. Although this is, in many ways, one of the most interesting, vigorous, and virile poems of the 1930s, its author later called it the worst failure of all his works, because it was based on a romantic communism which did not in fact exist.

In 1935 W. H. Auden published *Look, Stranger!* and attempted to force the reader to examine his society with a realistic and empirical eye. The same year C. Day-Lewis left behind some of the romantic ardor and the prescriptive fuzziness of *The Magnetic Mountain* to look more analytically at his world in *A Time to Dance*. There are at least two elements of transition from earlier works. In the first poem, "Learning to Talk," the poet rejoices that his little son will live in the better world that he is trying to build. *From Feathers to Iron* had traced the gestation and birth of a son to C. Day-Lewis. The other transition is the phrase "Start dancing now in town," from the last stanza of *The*

Magnetic Mountain. This may also be the genesis of the title "A Time to Dance," even though this dance is to a very different tune than the gay hopefulness of the previous work.

"Moving In" raises Day-Lewis's familiar problem of joining opposites. Coming down from the city to the country-side, just as one thinks it possible to join two worlds, urban and rural, old and new, he catches a vision of the death of the old world in shock, earthquakes, chasms, doom. So it is not a matter of connection, for one of the opposites is stark, cold dead, with no spark dancing between the area. In the world of private ownership no proudest possession should make the socially conscious man forget his indebtedness to anonymous workers, leaden arcs who might have been bright metal like himself, but instead content that the spark should dance between them and that they should die, burned out in the power's service. "Losers" continues with the same thought, but now more defined and delineated. What about the people of the past who made great efforts, but somehow missed the goal? They shall be transfigured into the present generation which now struggles against great odds. But what about all those who were born into such extreme poverty and deprivation that they owned nothing that could stand any test; falling apart before they reached maturity, they had no beauty in their rachitic bodies to lose? All they could do was to struggle for mere subsistence. When their children woke up in the morning, it was to a world worse than any nightmare. They built splendid cities as part of an anonymous labor force, but they were not ennobled by their work; it kept them barely alive, ambitious only for a crust of bread.

"In Me Two Worlds" rehearses the old conflict, but this time one more frequently described by W. H. Auden. The two worlds are past and future, and the poet is a "theatre of war." Although he belongs to both old and new, the rebel cells in his body call for the victory of new men and of a new world over the insolent power of the dead.

"A Warning to Those Who Live on Mountains" is a modern prophetic poem in the tradition of Jonah's warning—"yet forty days and Nineveh shall be destroyed." Those who live in the high, favored, privileged places of this present age have very little time left for the enjoyment of privilege. The people below grow impatient, the dynamite charge is laid, the hand to light it will not much longer hesitate. Then, instead of being like a mountain, their dwelling will resemble a condemned tenement. When the fall comes will they be adamant in their power, or will the tale tell about someone who changed his mind at the last moment, when it was too late to act?

One of the two more significant poems in the sequence is entitled "Johnny Head-In-Air," a name first used almost in passing in *Transitional Poem*. In *A Hope for Poetry* (1934) Day-Lewis uses "Johnny Head-In-Air" to illustrate the dilemma of any poet who loves the past but finds the future electric and creative. "So there arises in him a conflict; between the old which his heart approves and the new which fructifies his imagination; between the idea of a change of heart that should change society and the idea of a new society making a new man; between individual education and mass economic conditionment. At which end should one begin?" (chapter 8). It might be said that in treating such a topic the poet has no business to be trespassing; wandering into other people's fields, he must take the consequences. But the areas of proper function are not so simple as that. The poet, besides being a poet, is also a man, "fed with the same food, hurt with the same weapons" as other men. If there is hope in the air, he will sense it; where there is agony all about, he will suffer for it. What he feels as a man, he must reveal as a poet. It is just as absurd to tell him that he must feel strongly only about natural scenery as it is to call every nature poet an escapist. Nor should the poet be concerned only with the great eternal facts of summer and winter, birth, marriage, and death. Although these are indubitably mountain-peaks of human experience, they are also the background against which are measured such temporal things as the "rise and fall of cities, the year's harvest, the moment's pain." Today the foreground is fluid, confused, contradictory. Standing at the end of one age and reaching out toward another better age, the poet's arms are stretched toward opposite poles, the old life and the new; herein lies his power and his crucifixion.

> Come down, come down, you suffering man,
>
> .   .   .   .
>
> That cannot be till two agree
> Who long have lain apart:
> Traveller, know, I am here to show
> Your own divided heart.[8]

A man between two worlds, as a poet he is in an intolerable position. The Communist tells him that he is only a dope-peddler unless he "joins the revolution." Although the achievements of the "bourgeois" art of the past are undeniable and to be respected, the function of artists in the present crisis is to turn men's attention from the bourgeois past toward the proletarian future, to be propagandists for the new world. The bourgeois critic rebukes the poet for allowing a political sympathy with communism to drive him into a kind of writing that is not so much poetry as propaganda.

"Johnny Head-In-Air" depicts a vast horde of men who seek salvation trooping along an iron road, in the fall of the year. Approaching a distant mountain, they have come to a crossroads. A figure is stretched on a signpost. First he points to the right, the west (America), and says that this path leads to a pleasant low country, dying and dreaming in the late sun. To travel to the left, the east (Russia), the pilgrims must throw off their goods (abolition of private ownership) and their gods (atheism) and travel a long, hard way to reach the mountain of their goal. But once reached (cf. The Magnetic Mountain) they will all be friends and a society of equal men will be born.

Then, with a brilliant shift of imagery, the signpost becomes two electric poles, and instead of a string of lanterns, the poles are now united by the body of the man pulsing with the terrible electric current of contemporary man's crucifixion. The crowd is so moved by the plight and the speech of Johnny that they invite him to come down (cf. G. Studdert-Kennedy's "man on the cross") and travel with them. But his function is not to lead the crowd to the mountain; he hangs between the poles to serve society as the living emblem of one drawn two ways simultaneously who can find only the fusion of terrible suffering. The man on the posts serves to reveal to the men on the ground the dividedness of their own hearts.

If the question is raised about Johnny as a Christ-figure, there need be no hesitation in embracing both Day-Lewis's identification of Johnny as poet, and the obvious identification of him by the poem as crucified Christ. We have already pointed out the quasi-religious nature of Day-Lewis's attitude toward his poetic calling, one which we have called prophetic. Here clearly the poet is a prophet, reminding the people of their past misdeeds, pointing them to a better future, and bearing in his own body the sins of them all.

The other poems in A Time to Dance are variations on the main themes already introduced. "The Conflict" describes the peace of the poet when he used to fly above the clouds and stay out of the ring. But in this kind of a world even the pleasantest retreat is no longer possible; neutrality has never had the power to save. Although there seems to be no doubt in the poet's mind that the new socialism offers the only hope, yet he accepts that help reluctantly, and appears to have to keep convincing himself. However, such is the cyclical pattern of Day-Lewis's mind—delineate a conflict, then walk all around, viewing it from every possible angle—that mere repetition of a difficulty ought not necessarily to emphasize its intractability. "Moving In" is addressed to the modishly modern who refuse to be impeded by the lush growth of the past (yews) or held back by the rules of religion (churchyard emblems). But the poet warns them that now that they have cut a view to the stern hills, the message of those hills is not the old comfortable invitation of rooftops and spires, but a strict call to dedication.

The other significant poem is "A Time to Dance." An elegy to L. P. Hedges, the work has inserted into its middle a long narrative describing the flight of two aviators from England to Australia in 1920. Although the basis of the narrative is an actual experience, its use here is to illustrate the daring, improvisation, and gallantry of the kind of men who will lead others to the magnetic mountain. The exploit of lieutenants Parer and M'Intosh qualify them to join those superior individuals who will lead the way beyond the frontier to the unchartered promised land. Although there are almost no specifically political references, the temptation is overwhelming to attach the whole poem to *The Magnetic Mountain* as a definition of the brave breed that will inspire others to travel toward a healing new world.

The elegy has all the usual qualities of concern for the dead one's present existence and the relationships between life, death, and the total universe. The poet's concern that his friend should be within him is much like Tennyson's in *In Memoriam*, and other pantheistic solutions to the problem of death. His definition of true religion as joy in the heart reiterates the assertion of *The Magnetic Mountain*.

At the end of the poem, the writer is quite specific in calling for revolution as the only correct solution. Not only is it correct, but it's bound to win. And so it's a time to dance, not waiting for the individual utopian days that will come after worldwide socialist revolution. By this kind of lightheartedness the giant's roof will collapse and his walls come tumbling down. The poem is full of the masculine zest and drive of *The Magnetic Mountain*, swinging along with seldom a regret, capable of turning an elegy for a dead friend into an occasion for mirth and reassurance.

In 1936 C. Day-Lewis published his most political tract in the strange form of a verse drama entitled *Noah and the Waters*. With stunning use of religious archetype, he makes Noah a petty bourgeois who sees the threat of a working-class revolution before anyone else sees it (building his ark), and although all his property and his human ties bind him to the land and the solidarity of his fellow burgesses, in agony but certainty he makes his decision to float upon the waters. The waves, of course, represent the masses leaving their assigned traditional banks, flowing up over the solid land while the upper classes arm themselves with poison-gas outfits, shotguns, mops and buckets—against a tidal wave!

In the foreword, Day-Lewis explains that the work was conceived as the "book" for a choral ballet, but the author soon discovered that he was producing something like a modern morality play. He admitted that as it stands, *Noah and the Waters* is probably not suitable for the contemporary stage. He considered that the play derived its weight from the imminence of the issue it represented rather than from any of the more common dramatic techniques. Perhaps Thornton Wilder's highly dramatic and theatrical treatment of Noah's flood in *The Skin of Our Teeth* might have encouraged him to revise his fainthearted verdict. But the issue is entirely clear and thoroughly underscored—the choice of Noah whether to cling to the familiar old life of private property and class structure or to trust himself to the workers in their revolution to build a better world. The perfect epigraph for the drama was taken from *The Communist Manifesto*: "Finally, when the class war [the Flood] is about to be fought to a finish, disintegration of the ruling class and the old order of society becomes so active, so acute, that a small part of the ruling class [Noah and his family] breaks away to make common cause with the revolutionary class, the class which holds the future in its hands."

The prologue shows Day-Lewis's tendency to make nature poetry bear social significance, as the reader is invited to consider a piece of plowland as a graph of history, to recognize that it was the unregarded sweat of feudal serfs that made it fertile, to read between the furrows the desperate appeal of all those who earned only dire poverty from their labors, to hear young corn whisper the dreams of exploited tenant farmers who had absolutely no other voice. Certainly in this prologue, the unlikely juxtaposition of nature and politics is exceptionally adroit.

Besides the thematic considerations, the play is marvelously funny and satirical. For example, the three burgesses beg Noah to intercede with the waters for the sake of the town—meaning their own private business interests. Or for the sake of common humanity—meaning their own families. They attempt to bribe Noah with promises of power, a special job, high profits. Then the burgesses turn to the waves to flatter and bribe them; when flattery fails they turn to blustering threats, accusing their own serfs of being foreign elements. They raise again the myth of cooperation and tell the parable of a millstream that ruined a mill and thus lost it occupation. Finally they deliver their ultimatum: if the waters refuse to subside, they will call in waters from abroad, and when the flood-revolution is crushed, as punishment and to see that it never occurs again, the repressive burgesses will pave over all the streams and make them flow underground. Of course the obvious answer is for the silent waters of the world to flood together against repressive tyrants everywhere.

Noah accuses the burgesses of causing the revolution by their own follies. The action of the waves will rescue the earth, not ravish it. Then he proceeds to fill his ark with animal-virtues: mole-patience; salmon-courage, bullfinch-faith, monkey-curiosity, gannet-singlemindedness, sheepdog-wisdom. As the ark sheers away from the land, he looks at a lighted window in the home of the mistress he loved but with whom he could never share his questions or his dreams. Love will now be the strong clasp of the waves as they sustain his trusting keel.

This delightful drama ends with the usual prophetic utopian vision of a time when the flood waters will recede, when the raven (tenderness) and the dove (peace) emerge from the ark. As the waters wed the fertile valleys, the sun will bring forth the noble race that Noah had the faith to foresee behind the avenging veil of the raging waters.

The lines in which Noah is shown as a man who wishes to commit himself to neither side, a man who always sees both sides of every question, who hesitates to join a worker's uprising which will inevitably wipe out much of the cherished older way of life is a heart cry of Day-Lewis and Stephen Spender as they move toward Communism. The four poets of this study were united in a common diagnosis of the times and a common prescription for the redemption of time: Louis MacNeice saw the decay of the old and the ineffectiveness of contemporary liberalism, but could give communism only intellectual assent, not the vigorous affirmation of "the guts." Auden, distrustful of party cries and outside authority, and apparently shocked by the crisis that arose in the middle of the decade, simply became more insistent upon the need for moral response to coldly clinical judgments. As Day-Lewis and Spender searched their ailing world for a savior-figure, they could find nothing capable of withstanding the giant foe of fascism but the almost equally frightening friend communism. So that from about 1934–37 the four poets were in essential agreement that the times were out of joint and that something radical was needed to set them straight. But while MacNeice seemed stuck in a shell-pocked drain (*The Last Ditch*) and Auden was moving from materialistic pragmatism to the existential pragmatism of Kierkegaard, Spender and Day-Lewis were becoming disillusioned with the political program upon which they had set their hopes. An era of optimism for the future and confidence in the acts of the present was running out, and it was not yet clear what was to take its place.

Nevertheless, for his novel of 1937, *Starting Point*, Day-Lewis was still talking, in the terms of its epigraph, about the reluctant journey, hesitant and often looking back, which, when it reaches a certain point must continue to a new place of beginning: "From a certain point onward there is no longer any turning back. That is the point that must be reached" (Franz Kafka). The table of contents mirrored the same reluctant movement: Lost Causes; Knowledge of Necessity; The Point That Must Be Reached.

Like Day-Lewis, the hero Anthony Neale often finds his ideas and his experiences coming at him in terms of opposites: " 'I don't believe you can value anything properly till you've experienced its opposite, proved the comparative worthlessness of its opposite, if you like.' " [9] He wishes to commit himself irrevocably to some demand that life will make upon him, and the sooner the better. He expects to be a leader, but one who expresses in his own deeds and utterances the will of his group, not the egocentric individualism of a Napoleon or a Henry Ford. In the meantime he is content to merge himself into the anonymity of ordinary men. He makes the typical bourgeois, liberal mistake of attempting to create a model English village where at least a few hundred people can achieve a decent life, but his reforms are too trifling to make the radical breakthrough he desires. His father exemplified the judicial error. Achieving almost perfect disinterestedness, he deliberately cut off his intelligence from his emotions. His conservative friend John Henderson, capriciously discharged from a firm, is forced by circumstance to newfound economic indignation: " 'The horrible thing is that this should be able to happen at all,' said John. 'That people like Lewin, just because they own the means of production, should have this damnable power over the rest of us. And they're the people who make pretty speeches about the Dignity of Labour. Dignity! My God! When they know perfectly well that they can make us creep like worms in front of them for the privilege of earning their profits for them. Doesn't it make you sick?' " [10]

Another friend, Percy Appleton, urges him to jettison private scruples gained at the public schools of England and join with other revolutionaries in an underground insurrection. But before he can engage very effectively in domestic revolution, his conscience leads him to join the International Brigade to fight for the socialist government of Spain. Perhaps this diversion, which certainly occurred in the personal histories of many of the Oxford Poets' friends, is the weakest and most sentimental moment in the book. One senses that each enlistee in the international cause means one less worker in the social-economic revolution at home. The novel, like the poems, ends on the sentimental thought of comradeship and the prophetic vision of a utopia ahead: "Appleton, Grove, Sinclair, Morris: all the comrades; in streets, in the country, in prison, in factories, in the little room above the tobacconist's shop and the

May-Day Demonstration—they were with him and would be with him as long as he lived. These men and women—the oppressed, the anonymous, the workers—history had called them out of the ranks and given them her secret orders: they were the spies she sent forward into a hostile country, a land whose promise perhaps they alone could fully realize. . . . it was these hands, Anthony believed, which would guide a new world struggling out of the womb." [11]

Overtures to Death and Other Poems (1938) continues to investigate the unfortunate social condition of the present and to ferret out the escapists from social responsibility who must bear their share of the blame. But the utopian vision of a happy land about to be built has been completely displaced by the bitter urgency of warning. In the face of either the impending violence of the class struggle or another world war, the poet is desperately anxious to warn while there is still a tiny margin of time left. The inevitability of international ruin arouses in the poet a kind of furious anger and self-torment as he sees death so clearly and can find no viable hope for shielding himself and his generation. This anger sometimes finds its vent in accusation; other times in a kind of corrosive irony which is quite a new note in the poet's usual clean-cut, swinging lyricism.

The most powerful notes are struck by the poems in the first half of the volume; they are full of the presentiment of death. With his fondness for the eschatological touch on nature poems, in "Maple and Sumach" Day-Lewis sees the vivid leaf colors as the dying of light, and a sky on fire as warning to the world that it is about to die. With all of Spender's special compassion for little children, and his own parental concern as well, Day-Lewis, in "February 1936," is tormented in the midst of children's mirthful laughter to visualize how their blood will look on the street.

In "Bombers," the seeds of spring are already conceived in an "iron embryo" and now preparing for delivery. In *The Magnetic Mountain*, Day-Lewis had seen newspapers as the opiate of the people, drugging them against a clear vision of their world's sickness and against any remedial action. There the critique was jocular, exaggerated, jazzy. "Newsreel" has a different tone as it attempts to stab wide awake the habitués of "dream-houses." When they see the big guns rising up on the screen do they realize that their shells will fall on their own homes? Some night, doped by the movie, or sound asleep in the dark, they will stumble out the exit to face an air raid and the fragments of children flung about the wreckage. Then they will know that they have slept too long.

The title poem of the volume predicts the violence of a workers' revolution. In seven separate poems seven faces of death are portrayed. The first pictures the postwar generation of 1920 as attracted by death, seeking it in aeroplanes, fast cars, hospitals, and vice. But now that death is actively seeking them, they are no longer so attracted. A member of the upper classes sleeps in the handsome shell of his dead culture, fatalistically awaiting the great bailiff, death. The third poem accepts death because it is a natural force, but it cannot forgive the "criminal agents" of a waning will to live. In poem 4 death is asked to forgive such naïveté that its victims should have thought innocents might be exempt. And the poet restates the philosophic position which gives him the power to break out of fatalism and to act: man alone is responsible for creating the conditions of his life. Over death he may have little dominion, but over life only he can determine ways and means.

Three types of escape are delineated and rejected: natural determinism which denies man's freedom to shape his own world, visions of a better world which are hopelessly ineffective and naïve, the idea that society's health can be created by individual goodness. Auden too had warned the reader against weak private morality in a stirring public time in *Look, Stranger*. And something about the juxtaposition of the two poems and poets sets sharply in contrast Day-Lewis's bright incandescence by comparison with Auden's subterranean probing—an activity which the former delineates as mole-like in "Letter to W. H. Auden" (*From Feathers to Iron*):

A mole first, out of riddling passages
You came up for a breather into my field,
Then back to your engineering.

In "Sonnet for a Political Worker" (*Overtures to Death*), Day-Lewis reminds him that instead of getting worn out weighing alternatives, arguing, repeating the same old statements—calloused by the tricks of opponents and the fault-finding of friends, or trying to deal individualistically with history—he should be ministering to each man's individual need with patience, love, and warm inventiveness. In "Question," the main query is whether a person always needs to be forced by circumstances before he will be able to release himself into action. The poet's "Self-Criticism, and Answer" is somewhat surprising. For this lyric poet with a wholly natural and spontaneous singing voice bewails his meticulously "careful art" which he considers to have no power to storm the senses! He reasons that in a time of international madness, poets need such floods of indignation that they can dig channels in dry hearts and moisten up dry bones to live.

Although it falls beyond the delineated decade of this study, it is necessary to take a look ahead at *Word Over All* (1943) because it reveals such significant shifts in point of view. The epigraph is taken from Walt Whitman's poem "Reconciliation": "Word over all, beautiful as the sky, / Beautiful that war and all its deeds of carnage must in time be utterly lost, / That the hands of the sisters Death and Night incessantly softly wash again, and ever again, this soiled world."

Part 1 is made up entirely of new poems which have the passage of time as their theme. In part 2, it is the title poem that has particular interest. Amidst the flotsam of a wrecked world, what can the poet say, surrounded by abysmal hollows and crests of waves that show no land in sight? The poet has known personal sorrow and loss, but now millions flock down the road to oblivion. Searchlights, sirens, and bomb-strikes; how can one comfort the old man whose roof was blown off, the child buried beneath debris? Preachers and politicians have no hesitation to speak, and the poet feels the requirement upon him, for he has chosen to live with the violent present. But the Causes fade, and only humanity stands forth larger than before. "The Assertion" claims that at a time so full of mass murder, famine, shipwreck, when the whole earth winces at man's ill will, this is the time to assert once again that "men are love." "Watching Poet" (July 1940) memorializes the nights when, along with a neighbor farmer, Day-Lewis watched over the Axe Valley. Inevitably their conversation turned from war to crops and the hope that soon all would be peace and men and country could return to their natural occupations. Another war poem, "The Stand-To" (September 1940), named the men who have watched and waited with him. "Where Are the War Poets?" reflects the demand that poets write patriotic verse. But to do so would be to exchange their honest dreams of world-transformation for a quiet preference for the bad over against the worst. "Airmen Broadcast" expresses the shock of a time when men hunt men instead of the little creatures of field and forest. "Lidice" asks when the killer will see that he is aiming his sword at his own heart? "Ode to Fear" confesses that the "endemic guilt" of all men makes them accept fear as their due portion. "The Dead" claims that violent death has come as the resulting opposite to soft inaction and the retreat of dreams. "Reconciliation" plays Day-Lewis's old game of attempting to unite opposites. The mortal wound of a tank driver unites the past and the future that might have been, the world without and the world within. "Will It be So Again?" asks if it will happen all over again that the best will be lost and the empty schemers will go on to rebuild a lunatic world?

With the exception of "After the Storm," part 3 of the collection *Word Over All* is about the memory of the past. Even the one exception is about wartime in the past when men were bound together by mutual deeds of offense and defense. Now in the present they wander "vague and sluggish" down the boulevards.

Thus, although there are many poems about the tasks,

the deprivations of war, the difficulties of being a patriotic poet for a time and cause in which you do not wholeheartedly believe, there is almost nothing about the coming class war and the universal revolution, the utopian society, or magnetic mountains that draw all men to a city of brotherly comradeship. Indeed, as the poet said, the cause has waned and only a generalized concern for humanity is left.

2

Stephen Spender: The Proletarian Poet

In *Modern Poetry*, Louis MacNeice claimed that T. S. Eliot provided the *mise en scène* for his generation to play Hamlet against a background of the local gasworks. In the charming and revealing autobiography, *World Within World*, Stephen Harold Spender recalled that it was at Oxford he "started writing poems containing references to gas-works, factories, and slums." Thus he understood the significance beneath the affectation of Auden's dictum that the most beautiful walk in Oxford was along the canal, past the gasworks, where the poet must travel "dressed like 'Mr. Everyman.'" [1]

No doubt all three poets recalled, without troubling to make mention, that Rimbaud in the previous century had proclaimed the absolute necessity of being modern, and that in the previous generation Eliot had explicitly written poetry about broken springs in factory yards, fishing in the canal, and winter evenings spent behind the gashouse. So it is not surprising that, in an early poem "Acts Passed Beyond the Boundary of Mere Wishing" (*Poems*), Spender should speak of love in quantitative terms, demanding that if it were electrical energy it should be sufficient to run a factory, supply power for a whole city, or drive a train. Nor that he should extol the scream of express trains, permit the mechanical to triumph over the pastoral; nor that Day-Lewis should utilize railway imagery to signal the end of love; nor that MacNeice should see in the constant tearing up of the street before his apartment a presage of the disintegration of his era and the constant threat of war.

The critics quickly noted the departure from the diction of Georgian poetry with its glorification of tidy, domestic landscape, and Spender was given the dubious distinction of being considered the most urban and modern of the proletarian poets. His "Express" and "The Landscape Near an Aerdrome" say essentially the same thing: a train or a plane are really more significant in the life of modern man than the fields and farms his poetic ancestors had sung about.

Tennyson had moaned decorously over an English seaport where "Science grows and Beauty dwindles—roofs of slated hideousness!" Clearly this is one position open to the modern poet; he may tunefully deplore the pollution of the atmosphere and the spoliation of the land by the twin specters of science and industry. Or he may go farther back, ignore the inroads of modernity, and seek out unchanged peat houses and shepherds' crofts. But both of these positions put the poet out of effective touch with his own age. Spender turns both from the rural past and the lament for beauties spoiled to a future in which the train and the plane increasingly dominate the life of man.

In *The New Realism* (an essay originally delivered as a lecture to the Association of Writers for Intellectual Liberty), Spender masses his basic argument and its supporting evidence. He sees all the most advanced schools of literature and painting in the year 1939 in revolt against the realism of a Galsworthy novel, that is, the imitation in literature of certain aspects of middle-class life, the painting of portraits of people who can well afford to have their portraits painted, the careful selection from nature of those aspects which would seem beautiful to a middle-class mind. Refusing to interpret life at this level, artists have tended to become "subjective, introspective, abstract, fantastic, surrealist, mad"[2]—all because they refuse to write about the lives of people who do not seem to them to live, or to duplicate in art that basic philosophy which is ultimately interested only in personal privilege and material possession. Thus the artist illustrates in his works the conflicts or the harmony which he himself feels between his subjective life and the life of the outside world. If he seems often to turn away from that outside, objective life, it is out of his nausea and disgust with the social systems of his day.

But Spender argues that there is one social system that offers hope: "now the one contemporary philosophy which offers a profound and complete analysis of modern life is socialism, and that is undoubtedly why it is impossible to imagine a realism in art to-day which would not be revolutionary." [3]

However, Spender admits that communism presents the artist with a problem as well as an opportunity. Communism insists upon the overthrow of the bourgeoisie by the working class, and most artists come themselves from the bourgeoisie. The tradition of the middle class is so strong that even if a writer like D. H. Lawrence is born in the working class, when he writes, he attempts to provide himself with a middle-class environment. When a writer remains in his bourgeois background and tries to write about proletarian subjects, he tends to produce a "serious and superior kind of travel book . . . one which introduces into a culture something from outside that culture, a curiosity, a legend, an escape." To this problem Spender suggests only the revolutionary solution: "until there is a working-class audience with means and leisure to produce a culture of its own, existing in a classless society, working-class literature will remain a rather grim form of travel book, an interchange between Disraeli's 'two nations' into which capitalist societies are divided." [4]

This solution leads directly to an opportunity. The party program of communism undoubtedly appeals to some artists precisely because it offers them a basis of understanding and reaching that huge class of society which previously had been entirely cut off from their art. Thus when Spender considers the life and work of a working man, he turns in sincere admiration to the sheer power and pace of modern transportation. If "Landscape Near an Aerdrome" glorifies a plane above a church, it is simply in the tradition of Henry Adams's "Prayer to the Dynamo," a poem which had its genesis in the World Exposition at Chicago in 1900—a setting Spender would have found most sympathetic. Considering the veneration of the Virgin to be the motive power which raised the great eleventh and twelfth century cathedrals (cf. Spender's quantitative delineation of love as enough power to light a city), Adams finds the motive power of the twentieth century in a dynamo exhibited at the exposition. Specifically religious motivation is irrelevant and, in a sense, traitorous to the twentieth century. Thus Petra's fiancé in Spender's *Trial of a Judge* [5] calls the judge an imitator of Christ, with a thin sexless body, protruding ribs, and whip-weals on his sides. He is full of self-pity, but gives the people only the same gifts which flowed from Christ's side: blood, water, and death. By his death wish, Christ actually betrayed the humanity he might have saved.

"The Express" puts the machine above nature or God in terms of contribution to the life of man. Spender's novel, *The Backward Son*, expresses the same reliance of life upon machine in the touching scene of a desperately lonely boy at an English preparatory school lying in bed with a deep sense of failure and isolation. Suddenly he gets an idea; reaching his hand out cautiously from under the covers he extracts from his jacket pocket the big Ingersoll wristwatch his father gave him. He tucks it under his ear where it ticks loudly and lovingly. Lest one might think its significance was simply the love of the father-donor, Spender plants its tender consolation in the islands of jewels sustained by faithful wheels and seas of shining metal. "Love spread from the watch now warmed by his hands and moistened by his sweat and tears, through the orifice of his ear to his heart, equally faithful and ticking. The watch loved him. He fell asleep." [6]

In "Variations on My Life—the First," [7] he considers the human body to be less efficient than an aeroplane and somewhat like William Butler Yeats's golden nightingale of artifice—but with fleas and sins, and much to learn to accept and live with.

All this suggests the existence for Spender of a kind of "frontier," but rather more complex than for Auden, Isherwood, or MacNeice. To the latter writers, the frontier idea seems to have been inherited from T. S. Eliot and always signifies the last outpost of a moribund culture against a rising sea of barbarism. Although this is occasionally Spender's meaning, too, he also uses the image of a frontier as something which divides human from nonhuman, individual from the group, and the old world from the better new world that is coming. But the distinction clearly breaks down in such a poem as "The Pylons" (*Poems*), in which the poet, instead of closing his eyes to the hideous steel towers of a rural electrification system and concentrating on the soft green fields, glorifies the pylons and grants to them the future. And the nonhuman structure proves to be of the very highest social value, for rural electrification programs help create a new world of human equality (cf. "Not Palaces, an Era's Crown") as well as give to the group an early soubriquet—"The Pylon Poets."

World Within World contains a detailed, albeit indeterminate statement about how Spender became linked with other writers of the period in the minds of the critics. In 1932 the Hogarth Press published an anthology of poems, *New Signatures*, edited by Michael Roberts. A year later, Roberts edited a second volume entitled *New Country*, containing prose as well as poetry. Both anthologies revealed a socially conscious group of new young writers: W. H. Auden, William Empson, C. Day-Lewis, Rex Warner, William Plomer, A. J. S. Tessimond, John Lehmann, Julian Bell, and Stephen Spender. Although some of the writers had never met and others were barely acquainted, yet the entire group wrote with extraordinary unanimity about the end of the present society and the coming of a revolutionary new order.

Then in 1933 Auden published *Poems*; Spender published his *Poems*, and Day-Lewis published *The Magnetic Mountain*. Although the volumes bore striking differences, the social similarities were sufficient for the critics thereafter to link the names of Auden, Day-Lewis, and Spender as members of a kind of twentieth-century Scriblerus Club. Yet the talents involved were decidedly individual: Auden's intellectuality was always notable, as his mind set the world of observation in pattern and image, brilliantly conceived and dramatically executed. Although his settings were always in the observable world of sense impression, his imagery was generally taken from the nightmare material of the sub-conscious mind as it was being bared by the psychoanalysts of the period. And it was possible for him to combine these inner and outer worlds in tight cerebral apothegm, in parody of preceding poets, or in current dance-hall syncopation. Day-Lewis, like William Butler Yeats, was more deeply rooted in the traditions of British poetry. To the landscapes and diction of the Georgians, he added factory, slum, and machine, as well as the language of contemporaneity. His metrical regularity was impressive, and amidst the slightly tongue-in-cheek quality of Auden's jazz rhythms, his stern-ness of purpose and expression gave a sense of stature. Spender, on the other hand, called himself "an autobiogra-pher restlessly searching for forms in which to express the stages of my development." [8] Criticized for having no skill in the use of rhyme, he thereafter wasted time trying to use rhyme in order to prove the critics wrong.

The description of himself as an "autobiographer" sup-ports the possibility that two descriptions of protagonists in "The Cousins" and "The Burning Cactus" may be consid-ered portraits of the artist by the artist. The first is a bit idealized: "this Werner was bony with light hair, a dreamy look, overlaid with traces of anxiety in a certain fussiness of the brow, veiling the clear eyes and high forehead as wire netting overlays a grass lawn; he had altogether a too intense expression." [9]

The second is somewhat less idealized: "The refinedness of his features was purely external: small spots on the skin, a rubbed redness of the neck, a looseness of the lips, the overarched nostrils, and slightly bloodshot eyes showed places where the surface seemed already tarnished by some-thing altogether coarser and more violent which threatened in time to alter the whole face." [10]

The rather frequent references to persons of mixed Jewish-Gentile ancestry (Petra in *Trial of a Judge*, and Werner as well as Lord Edward's sons in "The Cousins") plus the

typical plot structure in which the hero is troubled by
latent or overt homosexual tendencies also strengthen an
autobiographical interpretation which is clearly permissible
since the author points to it as a central key to his work.

Although neither as impressive a gift nor so frequently
used as in Auden and MacNeice, parody is one of the
qualities that united Spender to the other members of the
group. The most hilarious example of this minor talent may
be found in *The Backward Son* when Miss Higgins over-
hears a dirty word spoken in the boy's dormitory: "Perhaps
it is a far, far better thing than any of you realize that while
I was walking down the end of the corridor to my room,
after saying good night to the small boys, I heard your
voices raised in such unseemly clamor that even had I shut
the door of my room I cannot doubt but that I would have
been disturbed. . . . I shall have to reserve any decision
whether or no I report this extremely serious matter to the
headmaster. The voice of Duty urges me to do so, but another voice, of Mercy, forbids me, because I fear the furious
indignation of a mind [the mind of the headmaster] which
has never harboured an unclean thought [the headmaster
loves to flog boys!] when he hears of this misdeed." [11]

Were there other reasons besides similarity of theme,
image, and diction that often linked the three poets in
critical mention? Probably the dominance of Auden should
be mentioned as a unifying factor, for MacNeice, Day-
Lewis, and Spender were deeply impressed by Auden and
therefore permitted echoes of the admired friend to bounce
back out of their own lines. Another link that Spender
mentions was the self-conscious rejection of the kind of
writing that had immediately preceded. "The writing of the
1920's had been characterized variously by despair, cynicism,
self-conscious estheticism, and by the prevalence of French
influences. . . it was consciously anti-political." [12] Although
during the First World War Osbert Sitwell and Siegfried
Sassoon satirized the war and in the postwar period turned
to left-wing politics, they both later abandoned political
faith and activity entirely.

To Spender, the generation of the twenties expressed the

exhaustion of a Europe in which all the old regimes were going to pieces and the emergent order was scarcely perceptible. The Georgian poets were pre-1914. The War Poets of 1914–18 were either killed in battle or so shell-shocked by the impact of war on a global scale that their talents never developed. The poets of the 1920s represented an elaborate retreat from politics and the real world. The poets of the 1930s represented a return to the objective world outside and the recognition of the importance of the things men do together in groups: political action, social structure, cultural development.

Spender mentions the writers and artists of the Bloomsbury set as the most constructive and creative influence on the English cultural scene between the two wars. The names most frequently associated with this group were Virginia Woolf, Roger Fry, Lytton Strachey, Clive Bell, Vanessa Bell, Duncan Grant, Raymond Mortimer, and perhaps David Garnett. E. M. Forster and T. S. Eliot may be described as guests within the group rather than belonging to it.

The sacred dogma of Bloomsbury included French impressionism and post-impressionism in literature, agnosticism in religion, liberalism with socialist leanings in politics. Thus Eliot was too orthodox in religion and too conservative in politics to fit completely. Forster was too mystical, too moralistic, and perhaps too impishly unpredictable. In a way, Bloomsbury represented "the last kick of an enlightened aristocratic tradition." [13]

When Stephen Spender was preparing *Collected Poems: 1928–1953*, he felt under "an obligation to 'own up' to those poems, like . . . *The Funeral*, which, when they were written, provided a particular label for some of the poetry of the 'Thirties: an embarrassment to my friends' luggage more even than to my own' " (Introduction). The poem to which he confesses is a rather sentimental elegy to an unnamed and anonymous worker who excelled everyone else in making driving belts. The gathering is a festive time of statistical comparison when his comrades record the contribution of one "unit" to the cooperative whole. They lay his body in the earth and walk home with the Communist dramaturgy of red banners and party songs, and conversation about the Communist ideal of a world state with towns for brain centers. The single individual is always seen as part of a larger whole, one "cog [sic]" in a "golden hive," one spark from the total fire. When its task is "happily achieved" it quietly falls away. Individual grief is no longer a factor nor are tears shed, "crocodile" or genuine, for the great past of a dying culture.

This is fulsome even if naïve praise and rigidly follows the party line: one wins significance from the contribution of his labor to the greater good of the whole. Personal happiness arises out of working wholeheartedly for the ideals of world communism. The only reference to non-Communists is in such invidious terms as "haunted," "crocodile tears," "decline of a culture," "ghosts of Greek boys."

A somewhat similar Communist elegy is to be found in *Trial of a Judge,* when Petra's brother, dying for the cause, comforts his sister-in-law. No one is to judge his life of martyrdom as unhappy. He built his life into the foundation of that new world which will contain happiness. Both his peace of mind and his material interests were sustained by his belief in the brotherhood of man. G. S. Fraser commented upon Spender's sympathy with those who experience "self-pity rather than stoicism, weakness rather than strength, failure rather than success." [14] But Spender would have replied that his weak heroes are truly successful—they are building the new world! The poem "Easter Monday" (*The Still Centre*) depicts the bourgeois dressed in tweeds, wearing gold-framed glasses which focus on the velvety far-off mountains. But the working men hold up the future world in the midst of the falling-away of the effete present.

Vienna (canto 3) describes the making of a Socialist. Wallisch, a Socialist hero and martyr became a mason's apprentice at the age of eleven. Exploited by employers as a child, by sixteen he had become only an assistant mason. At seventeen wandering through Austria and Germany, he saw everywhere the oppression of workers by bosses. By 1905 he joined the Communist party and his experience in

World War I, where he served with distinction, confirmed his resolve to remain a Socialist until he died.

Returning to Vienna returns also to the same martyr, now representative of men who turned away from dogma about the soul and hammered out a better world where workers would think they were in heaven. The shelled Karl Marx Hof crushed within its ruins dead workers like fallen angels about whom all the old apocalyptic language might be spoken: their tears were pearls, their cheeks golden, and when the tears splashed to the pavements, they turned to bright diamonds. So the depiction of the Socialist worker has run the gamut from a unit in a large machine, through political force, to a secular saint and martyr.

By comparison, none of the other selections from *Poems* and *The Still Centre* sound quite so enthusiastic. "In 1929" (*Poems*) arose out of a personal friendship during a trip to Germany. A German youth, Joachim, invited Spender to a walking trip along the Rhine. En route Joachim picked up Heinrich, who became "the greatest attachment of his [Joachim's] life." The latter represented the workless wanderers of 1929 Germany, born in war, starved during the blockade, stripped of cash by the inflation. "I wrote a poem in which I described the young bank clerk with 'world-offended eyes'" who stood naked with the "new German," and preparing to build his new world "out of our bones." [15] Similarly "Oh Young Men, Oh Young Comrades" (*Poems*) counsels youth, the "new Germans," to desert the houses their fathers built and to "rebel!" In "An Elementary School Classroom in a Slum" (*The Still Centre*), the poet-teacher suggests that to expose slum children to the culture of the upper classes is simply an invitation to revolution.

When Stephen Spender was visiting in Berlin with Christopher Isherwood, the latter received a letter from his best friend of Cambridge days (whom he called Chalmers in the autobiographical sketch *Lions and Shadows*) confessing that he had joined the Communist party. Both young men regarded this as an extraordinary step to take. When Chalmers arrived in Berlin, on his return to England from an Intourist tour of Moscow, he turned out to be much like the smiling young Comsomol hero who saves boys in a reform school in one of the group's favorite Russian films, *The Way into Life*. As Spender and Chalmers walked through Berlin together, the pressures of the city, the widespread unemployment, the ideology of fascism, and the danger of war gave their conversation poignant relevancy. Isherwood described (1931) Berlin as "in a state of civil war. Hate exploded suddenly, without warning, out of nowhere; at street corners, in restaurants, cinemas, dance halls, swimming-baths; at midnight, after breakfast, in the middle of the afternoon. Knives were whipped out, blows were dealt with spiked rings, beer-mugs, chair-legs or leaded clubs; bullets slashed the advertisements on the poster-columns, rebounded from the iron roofs of latrines. In the middle of a crowded street a young man would be attacked, stripped, thrashed and left bleeding on the pavement; in fifteen seconds it was all over and the assailants had disappeared. . . . And morning after morning, all over the immense, damp, dreary town . . . young men were waking up to another workless empty day." [16]

Chalmers felt that Europe was bound to be destroyed by a war between reborn German nationalism supported by American and British capitalism, and socialist Russia. How could this be prevented? "I gave my stumbling answers: I desired social justice; I abhorred war; I could not accept dictatorship and methods of revolutionary violence." Chalmers listened quietly, and when Spender had finished speaking, replied only the one word, " 'Gandhi.' " [17]

It was at this point in time and personal development that Spender found his vaguely distressed consciousness beginning to formulate arguments along the Marxist line. It is certainly quite clear that after this time Spender believed that communism offered the only workable analysis and solution of complex world problems, that it was sure eventually to win, and that for significance and relevance the artist must somehow link his art to the Communist diagnosis. It was an era in which sensitive persons became painfully aware of great social injustices—on the national level the oppression of one class by another, on the international level the colonialism, political or economic, practiced by one nation upon another. At home and abroad, a contemporary critic indicted, there was "mass unemployment through the world, workers' poverty in homes, humbug from famous people, the all-importance of money in worldly estimates of worth, the lack of meaning in accepted creeds."

Against this universal guilt, of which the poet felt a part, "Communism, or Socialism in its completed form, offers a just world—a world in which wealth is more equally distributed, and the grotesque accumulation of wealth by individuals is dispersed; in which nations have no interest in destroying each other in the manner of modern war, because the system of competitive trade controlled by internecine and opposed capitalist interests is abolished." [18]

Not only did communism seem the only feasible answer, it was the one which must prevail. Third Red (*Trial of a Judge*, act 5) argues that since the innumerable working people dig the metal to forge their own fetters and build the planes which will drop bombs on their Socialist apartment houses, they have only to use their mountainous power of numbers to overwhelm their few oppressors. In the final confrontation of the drama, Black Fascists against Red Communist, the Red Chorus insists doggedly that in spite of the apparent immediate successes of the Fascists, the future—free and peaceful—belongs to them. *Vienna* (canto 4) likens the workers to insects building cells underneath a monstrous shell of ruins. They support the empty shell momentarily; their work even alters its conformation; but at last, what they have built in justice and brotherhood will bring the whole husk tumbling down.

Spender's prophecy of the coming victory of world socialism in poem, drama, and prose brings us inevitably to the question of the relationship between communism and the life and work of the artist. Spendor quotes, with only partial approval, the principles dictated by Auerbach, a young representative of the bureaucracy to the Kharkov literary congress, a meeting of Communist writers from every part of the world. (1) Art is a class weapon. (2) Artists are to abandon "individualism" and their fear of strict "discipline" as petty bourgeois attitudes. (3) Artistic creation is to be "collectivized," and carried out according to the plans of a central staff like any other soldierly work (4) This is to be done under the "careful and yet firm guidance of the Communist Party." (5) Artists and writers of the rest of the world are to learn how to produce proletarian art by studying the experience of the Soviet Union. (6) Every proletarian artist must be a dialectical materialist. (7) Proletarian literature is not necessarily created by the proletariat; it can also be created by writers from the petty bourgeoisie, and one of the chief duties of the proletarian writer is to help the nonproletarian writers "overcome their petty bourgeois character and accept the viewpoint of the proletariat." [19]

When such principles were applied to Spender and his friends he considered it intolerable, a more complete censorship than had been applied anywhere else in the world, for not content with banning books after they had been written, it would "order the manner in which books should be written, what they should be about, and what attitude the writer should adopt to his subject." [20] In July 1934 an article appeared in the *New Masses* attacking Auden, Day-Lewis, and Spender as aristocrats, aesthetes, and counterrevolutionaries. Nevertheless the thesis of *The Destructive Element* is that outside reality is the destructive element which the artist must not reject in favor of the golden poetic past, nor exchange for some escape from social reality into personal idiosyncrasy, but must immerse himself in, dangerous though it be, in order to practice a modern, significant, and revolutionary art.

A consideration of Spender's defense of the role of the artist in communism is incomplete without mention of his poem "To a Spanish Poet," Manuel Altolaguirre.[21] The poem is based on an incident reported in *World Within World*:[22] during an air raid a bomb fell upon Altolaguirre's home, making a stucco pigeon from the carved gable revolve in the air and say "Coo." Everything in the room was destroyed, but Altolaguirre was unharmed. The poem begins with the question of Altolaguirre's survival in the Spanish

Civil War and ends with the sentiment that even if the Spanish poet is dead, perhaps that solid corpse is built into a more lifelike structure of society than the spinning, revolving, dying world.

Writing an introduction to *Poems for Spain,* Spender pointed out that the volunteer principle of the International Brigade was matched by the nature of this collection of poetry, for many were written by men for whom poetry scarcely existed before the Spanish war. Some of these men, their gift for poetry aroused by the struggle, died in it before their talents had a chance to mature. Of course in any war, the battlefield becomes the heart of the organism, and thus any poetic tenderness concerning the body may have to express itself in terms of ambulances and sandbags. But the essential connection between poetry and Spain was that many writers sensed that the struggle there would decide whether or not free poetry could find any place in the coming world order. Thus Auden mused that tomorrow the younger poets might walk by the lake and spend weeks of perfect communication with friends, but today is the time to fight.

To such writers the Spanish war, as Keats said of Peterloo, was "No contest between Whig and Tory—but between Right and Wrong." Just as Spender reacts to contemporary Spain crushed by fascism, so, in William Wordsworth's sonnet "Indignation of a High-Minded Spaniard," the English Liberal tradition reacted to a Spain crushed by Napoleon:

Spain may be overpowered, and he possess,
For his delight, a solemn wilderness,
Where all the brave lie dead. But, when of bands
Which he will break for us, he dares to speak,
Of benefits, and of a future day
When our enlightened minds shall bless his sway;
Then, the strained heart of fortitude proves weak;
Our groans, our blushes, our pale cheeks declare
That he has power to inflict what we lack strength to bear.

Auden's *Spain* falls quite within the tradition of the Wordsworth sonnet. It might be called "academic poetry" in the sense that although Auden had been in Spain, the events of the poem are carefully distanced to indicate their significance to the spectator outside Spain. Spender's poems on Spain convey an immediate sense of the urgent doom lurking there. MacNiece's section on Spain in *Autumn Journal* is the confession of a tourist who enjoyed the trippers' sights, tried to ignore the sullen faces and the threatening graffiti, but now recognizes that no one in the world can afford to ignore Spain.

At this period in his life, instead of feeling that there are problems for the poet who is deeply involved in political activity, Spender considered that the problem is for the poet who is uninvolved. Werner, in "The Cousins," has the complacent sense that he represents "international Socialism and the arts, in fact he had the exhilirating sense that he, as the New World, rather added tone to the Old." [23] In his beautiful and perceptive chapters on Henry James in *The Destructive Element*, Spender explores the problem of the artist who refuses to accept objective reality: "His unwillingness to face certain aspects of reality may partly explain the withdrawal of his art from the objective world, until he had created a world of his own, in which it was possible for that reality to appear either in a form in which it was beautifully accepted (as in *The Ambassadors*), or in which it was 'shown up' in its full horror." [24]

Spender succinctly states his position in regard to political activity, the Spanish war, propaganda, and individualism in the foreword to *The Still Centre*: "As I have decidedly supported one side—the Republican—in that conflict [Spanish Civil War], perhaps I should explain why I do not strike a more heroic note. My reason is that a poet can only write about what is true to his own experience, not about what he would like to be true to his experience." Spender recognized that there was a certain pressure of external events exerted on poets of his era which made them tend to write outside their own experience. This was partly because the violence of the times and the necessity of sweeping and immediate action tended to dwarf the experience of the individual, and perhaps even to make his immediate environment and occupation things that he was ashamed of.

Not only was Spender not always sure of the solution of communism, there were times in his art when he was distinctly critical, or at least questioning. In 1935, he flatly stated: "The real objection to the Communist ideology in writing is that it is not self-critical. All it demands from a writer is that he should be a good [cf. C. Day-Lewis's sonnet "Yes, why do we all, seeing a communist, feel small? That small"] and explicit exponent of Communism: if he is that, it not only shields him from criticism; there is positively no ground on which it can criticize him." He points out that when Communists, in *New Masses*, and *International Literature*, criticize proletarian literature, they can attack the writer only ideologically. Thus a heavy-footed criticism in the *New Republic* of a picture book by Soglow begins: " 'Whether it is humor or not, depends entirely on the class point of view. . . . The question is whether the book is satire for the working class or superficial cartoons to amuse the well-to-do.' " If the writer is ideologically sound, Communist reviewers express the most naïve surprise that his book is not readable, and extend the most heartfelt hopes that proletarian writers will soon do better. "I imagine that to the perfect Communist literary critic it must be a matter of almost dumbfounded astonishment that a Chinese coolie who is a member of the party, cannot write books far better than the bourgeois propaganda of Shakespeare." [25]

Three years later, in *Trial of a Judge*, Spender permits the Fascist chorus (the Black Prisoners) to refer to Communists as machines without a nation, millions of bodies all the same, millions of minds which are without personal color, as unindividualistic as an Asiatic plain. The next year, 1939, in "The Bombed Happiness" (*The Still Centre*), the poet criticizes the education of children, for whom he seemed always to feel a special compassion. Their smiles are crystal, their leaping embrace gold; they wear happiness frankly, but society forces them into an unnatural mold. The world's tyrannical heart corrupts their trustfulness, drowns their rivers of song, and tramples their buffoonery. The "expanding state" finally buries gaiety, jest, play, and human happiness. The key phrase "expanding state" strongly suggests that although this is a criticism of education in the present capitalistic society, it could as easily be applied to the children reared under state socialism.

The New Realism, published the same year, closes with a twofold examination of the work of Christopher Caudwell. At first Spender discusses his "remarkable" book, *Illusion and Reality*, in a generally agreeable tone. He seems to agree that an artist must identify with the working class and write by the ideals of the future. But in a discussion of Caudwell's next book, *Studies in a Dying Culture*, Spender condemns Caudwell's advice as worthless. Caudwell, writing about G. B. Shaw, places him beside Wells, Lawrence, Proust, Huxley, Russell, Forster, Wassermann, Hemingway, and Galsworthy, as "men who proclaim the disillusionment of bourgeois culture with itself, men themselves disillusioned and yet not able to wish for anything better or gain any closer grip of this bourgeois culture whose pursuit of liberty and individualism led men into the mire. Always it is their freedom they are defending. This makes them pathetic rather than tragic figures, for they are helpless, not because of overwhelming circumstances but because of their own illusion."

But Spender insists that Communists must learn that writers who have entirely different ideological positions may sometimes make true critiques of reality. "The fundamental weakness of Caudwell's position is in assuming that the writer who is in a divided position is not in a position to portray historic truth. . . . It would be absurd to wish that Chekhov had joined the working-class movement. If he had, his work would not have been the body of literature we know. Yet Chekhov's descriptions of the 'pathetic' situations of people whom he loved and with whom he may have identified himself, the great truthfulness of his analysis of their lives, combine to make him a writer of historic importance, as well as a revolutionary writer who was sensitive to the decay of the society in which he lived. The pathos which Caudwell condemns is the writer's response to a world which was dying; it is their contribution to what we know of reality in our time." [26]

The Backward Son revealed the tendency of even the
most pitiable of the oppressed to seize their chance to become oppressors, thus indicating an erosion of idealism in
the role of the working man as savior. Geoffrey had never
dared to challenge the tyranny of Palmer and Richards, the
leading senior men of his school; he was even sycophantic
to the disgusting and unpopular Fallow and Like. But when
his beloved younger brother Christopher arrives at Tisselthorp House, he exerts tyranny over him. And the shocking
factor is that this tyranny is based not on competitiveness
in sports or academic subjects, but on the intimacy of love.
It would hardly be a step forward for the world to extend
to the proletariat the tendency of the oppressed to oppress
in their turn. Becoming masters, they would be masters
indeed!

Spender's ultimate statement of allegiance appears in his
autobiography: "Today, we are constantly told that we must
choose between the West and the East. . . . I am for
neither West nor East, but for my self considered as a self
—one of the millions who inhabit the earth." Thus Spender
does not so much choose America or Russia; he simply
judges between them. And if it seems absurd for a mere
individual to set himself up as judge between vast powers,
armed with all their superhuman machines of destruction,
then the poet can only reply "that the very immensity of
the means to destroy proves that judging and being judged
does not lie in these forces. For supposing that they
achieved their utmost and destroyed our civilization, who-
ever survived would judge them by a few statements, a few
poems, a few *témoignages*, surviving from all the ruins, a
few words of those men who saw outside and beyond the
means which were used and all the arguments which were
marshalled in the service of those means." [27]

It is apparent that Stephen Spender's diagnosis of the
present and his prognosis for the future were grounded on
a massive disappointment with the world, a disenchantment
felt by Matthew Arnold in the dichotomy of "Dover Beach"
between youthful dreams and reality, and more recently by
the French existential theater which defines absurdity as

the abyss between what we were taught to expect from the world and what we actually receive. The nausea to which it reduced the French writers was also experienced by Stephen Spender. Perhaps the most thoroughgoing example of this disillusionment is found in Geoffrey Brand, fictitious hero of *The Backward Son*, a novel which Spender's autobiography makes clear is anything but fictitious.

At nine, Spender became a boarder at Old School House Preparatory School, Gresham's School, Holt, because his marvelously efficient brother Michael had shone so brilliantly there. But when Stephen meets Michael at school, the latter tells him to call him Spender Major and explains firmly that they cannot often be seen together. At the school there developed a kind of symmetry whereby the upward curve of Michael was completed by the downward curve of Stephen. On a General Knowledge Paper set for the whole school, the name Spender Major appeared at the top of the list with ninety percent correct answers; the name of Spender Minor at the very bottom with five-tenths of one percent. The younger boy was violently homesick; he could not taste food; he could not focus on the contemporary scene; his mind was filled with overpoweringly sweet images of home. The worst moment of every day was waking, imagining he was in his own room at home and discovering with revulsion that he was still at school.

The headmaster at Gresham was the great Howson who stands revealed in both novel and autobiography as a petty tyrant. Fathers, he shouted, who did not beat their children were not men; boys who were not beaten by their fathers could never become men. The best favor one could do for a boy was to flog him systematically. To that glimpse of a pre-Dickensian world, can be added the hunger of the small boys who one day during the morning break at eleven o'clock, ate, not only their own quarter slice of bread, but also several quarters belonging to the older boys who had not yet arrived. The housemaster, Dr. Wynne Wilson, proclaimed that such an offense was beyond his capacity to punish; he must turn the culprits over to the boys themselves. Thus Spender was tied with rope and pulled at hands and feet in opposite directions (no doubt defended as increasing the height!), then flung down a hole at the back of the platform of the school dining room which contained at the bottom a layer of discarded kipper heads. The age of nine is young for such trauma, but it hardens the youth's defenses as he prepares to meet an inimical and hateful world.

The poems of the period 1930–40 express much the same disenchantment as the prose. The poem "What I Expected" (*Poems*) is a precise study of the literature of the absurd: I expected thunder, fighting, and climbing; instead I find graduality, fading, and the attrition of time; but I continue to search for brightness and innocence. Men who are in jail ("The Prisoners" [*Poems*]) have actually been in the jail of an inimical environment all their lives. In a world in which the oppressor deprives the poor, let there be no quietism of despair, nor any transformation of art or the peace of religion—let the raw sounds cry out in railway stations and on the street corners ("In Railway Halls, on Pavements Near the Traffic" [*Poems*]). Is there a changing point in human history which permitted heroes of the past to dream clearly and to act decisively, whereas men of the present are doomed to know only distraction and wavering uncertainty ("Exiles from Their Land, History Their Domicile" [*The Still Centre*])? But even if one were sure of his own mind what could he do in a war-torn world ("Who Live under the Shadow of a War" [*Poems*])? The entire trick, in such a time, is to escape the statistics of those lost in battle and to avoid the obituary columns at home ("Thoughts During an Air Raid").[28] The men who fight the war hate it thoroughly; they fraternize with the foe and are kept fighting only by the iron discipline of the revolver in an officer's hand ("Two Armies").[29] A young man should have the privilege of silly jokes and laughter, but there he lies dead ("Ultima Ratio Regum").[30] Knowing some of the dead personally, Spender dedicates "A Stopwatch and an Ordnance Map"[31] to Samuel Barber, a friend killed in action. The cowardly in battle die with a moment of cynical self-consciousness in which they realize that they were prepared for the bullets that killed them by the kisses of their own mothers and their sweethearts ("The Coward").[32]

The drama *Trial of a Judge* bristles with reference to the wound the world's reality inflicts on the sensitive. The cities decay, grass grows between rusting tracks of suburban lines; the unemployed lie idly on canal banks, sit in cafes, and fight in slum alleys. It is out of such unemployment, disgust, and violence that nazism flowers. Its blossoms are the kind of prejudice which finds the whole outside world guilty because at birth they are inferior, qualitatively, biologically, and metaphysically to the master race.

The collection of novella, *The Burning Cactus*, keeps repeating the pattern of individual lives which mirror in the small the vast malaise of their age. The heroine of "The Dead Island" was delivered to that place and condition by aeroplanes, liners, drink, drugs, love affairs, and the unforgivable loss of her cash. As Carlyle put it, the "cash nexus" is the significant key to a relationship in which she gives her young lover a banknote to pay for dinner. He accepts it unquestioningly, and does not even remember to give her the change.

It's a world in which the ruling order prides itself on stupidity. In "The Cousins" the aristocrats are ashamed of intellect: " 'Oh, brains, brains! Don't you see how Mummy and us do everything we can to cover up the fact that Daddy's so beastly clever. . . . none of the other peers are a bit brainy, really.' " [33] The life which George Meredith satirized so bitterly, Helen mistakes for the model life in "The Cousins": " 'They could ride before they could walk. . . . You may think it stupid, but, really, the life of a gentleman is a work of art. Do you read Meredith? In his books he describes the kind of life which seems to be the only life worth living.' " [34] And again Helen sings mistaken praises to Meredith: " 'More brain, oh Lord, more brain! Have you ever read *Modern Love?* You should do so. Where the brain is wanted is not in our books, our art, our commerce, but in our lives, our happiness—then you see, with the achievement of our life we can judge the world of mere *things*, books, business, pictures, churches. I'm sure that's what Edward meant last night when he said he judged life by standards he had acquired at Oxford.' " [35] Then making the whole thing warmly personal, she touched his arm, and he found himself becoming a moral lesson, an illustration of the world which she rejected. " 'Money,' she went on, 'one needs money to do all this, and then one can help the poorer people.' " [36]

The Destructive Element considers this to be a world without belief of which the best description is T. S. Eliot's *The Wasteland.* The importance of the dollar is itself an expression of the decadence of the time. "Money is in these novels [of Henry James] the golden key that enables people to live in a world where they are free to plot their lives beautifully, and to act significantly." Although Spender recognized that James had been severely criticized for his materialist view, he points out that there is a certain confusion in this criticism, because one has only to read James's letters to realize that the whole business of money and money-making disgusted him. "It simply struck him as a part of the moral incongruity and decadence of the world he was studying, that without this stained and dishonoured money, a life that was civilized and intelligent was practically impossible." [37]

This critical point of view converted many to socialism and was commonly held by liberal, cultured people before the war. It is clearly one of the basic themes of E. M. Forster's novel, *Howards End.* This sense of the importance of money coupled with political despair may have led inevitably to World War I: "beneath the stylistic surface, the portentous snobbery, the golden display of James's work, there lurk forms of violence and chaos. His technical mastery has the perfection of frightful balance and frightful tension: beneath the stretched out compositions there are abysses of despair and disbelief; *Ulysses* and *The Waste Land."*

James's images of suffocation, of broken necks, of wailing, most strongly resemble a collection of photographs of the dead and wounded during the war. They remind us of his phrase, spoken in 1915: "to have to take it all now for what the treacherous years were all the while really making for and *meaning*, is too tragic for any words." [38] It is the intense dissatisfaction with modern political institutions which has driven many writers into one form or another of subjectivism. "Joyce seems to me a religious artist. After his gigantic effort to impose epic values on the modern world, accepted even at its most sordid, he had been compelled not only to invent subjective symbols, but to invent a new language. The same kind of subjectivism, though in an elaborately disguised form, exists in Wyndham Lewis's most ambitious novel, *The Apes of God*." [39]

Dissatisfaction with the world tended to focus on the struggle of the Spanish Republicans. Spender was in Vienna, July 1936, when he first read the newspapers about the beginnings of the Spanish Civil War. He often discussed it with a group of Socialists who had been driven underground by the liquidation of the Austrian Socialists under the Dollfuss government in February 1934. But within a few weeks Spain became the symbol of hope for all anti-Fascists. Here was an indigenous cause which represented freedom and justice opposing a reactionary group. It was a real contest of ideas, not the usual seizure of a weak nation by dictatorial powers. Fascism, communism, and the liberal-socialism of world intellectuals were all finding voice in the great international debate about Spain. By contrast the worst feature of the Hitlerian successes was the way capitalistic politicians blindly did his work for him. Thus one day, the democratic statesmen who served him in a futile hope of preserving world peace had to accept elections in Austria and the Saar, directed by Hitler although disguised as expressions of the free will of the people; to recognize the Anschluss and the seizure of Czechoslovakia to correct the map of Europe; and to deny a truth they knew perfectly well, that British ships during the Spanish Civil War were sunk by Italian submarines in the Mediterranean.

Spender visited Spain in the summer of 1937 as a delegate to the Writers' Congress held in Madrid, even then under shell fire. The public purpose of the congress was to discuss the attitude of the intellectuals of the world toward the

Spanish war. But the private theme was Stalinists versus André Gide. "Gide had just published *Retour de l'U.R.S.S.* in which he had made a detached and critical account of his impressions of a tour of Russia, where he had been the honoured and flattered guest of the Soviet government. Far more sensational than the book itself was the fury with which it was received by Communists. Gide, who, only a few weeks previously, had been hailed in the Communist press as the greatest living French writer come to salute the Workers' Republic, became overnight a 'Fascist monster,' 'a self-confessed decadent bourgeois,' and worse. . . . The Congress with all its good qualities, had something about it of a Spoiled Children's Party, something which brought out the worst in many delegates." [40]

The hopes of intervention by men of good will in behalf of peace and world socialism collapsed with the victory of Franco in the Spanish Civil War. At the same time came the Munich settlement and the occupation of Czechoslovakia. As the fall of the Spanish Republicans marked the end of an era, the other events were the beginning of another war.

Not only was the world sick, according to Spender and other intellectuals of his period, but the vague good will of liberalism was without healing power. Love is not enough, the Judge (*Trial of a Judge*) says, unless it can supply enough power to run a whole country, a sentiment Spender had already expressed in "Acts Passed Beyond the Boundary of Mere Wishing" (*Poems*). Petra's mother states the matter even more categorically in the fifth act. She considers that both her martyred sons died for the sake of personal vanity. Justice has no power to overthrow human injustice. They loved human justice, and the most unjust, the most violent won. The Judge laments that at one time justice, although only seen with the inner eye of the mind or conscience, was just as solid and real as a table or a chair. But now everything crumbles, grows as invisible as real furniture relegated to an attic. Although it is the Black Prisoners (Fascists) who say it, there can be no question that Spender is contrasting the strength of fascism with the weakness of liberalism: The Nazis have shown how power can be used. Yet the Judge has a second thought, that although violence may win temporarily, when the liberal refuses to return violence for violence (cf. Jesus' Sermon on the Mount), he plants within his own refusal the seed of a better world.

Stephen Spender seems almost to be answering his own Judge when he states the thesis of *Forward from Liberalism*: "I argued that Liberals must reconcile Communist social justice with their liberal regard for social freedom, and that they must accept the methods which it might be necessary to use in order to defeat Fascism." In the preceding decade (the 1920s), there had been a generation of American writers—Scott Fitzgerald, Ernest Hemingway, Malcolm Cowley, and others, whom Gertrude Stein had called the "lost generation." Spender, as an anti-Fascist writer, lived in what has been called the pink decade, therefore was not part of the preceding lost generation. But artists even in that decade of social consciousness were divided between literary vocation and an urge to save the world from fascism. Thus, on the negative side, they were the divided generation of Hamlets who found the world out of joint and failed to set it right.[41]

William Wordsworth, at the beginning of the French Revolution, felt that the artist's chief duty was simply to survive in order to bear literary witness:

> *Doubtless, I should have then made common cause*
> *With some who perished; haply, perished too,*
> *A poor mistaken and bewildered offering,—*
> *Should to the breast of Nature have gone back,*
> *With all my resolutions, all my hopes,*
> *A Poet only to myself, to Men*
> *Useless, and even, beloved Friend! a soul*
> *To thee unknown!*
>
> (*The Prelude*, book 10, lines 229–36)

Spender's reply to Wordsworth's elaborate evasion of involvement would have reaffirmed the impulse to act. Generally the deeds of poets were the half-and-half actions of people divided between their artistic and their public conscience, and unable to fuse the two. "I now think that what I should have done was either throw myself entirely into political action; or, refusing to waste my energies on half-politics, made within my solitary creative work an agonized, violent, bitter statement of the anti-Fascist passion." [42]

But the signal problem of liberals with the Popular Front came into the open at a meeting in Tangier. It was the question of atrocities that most deeply disturbed Spender and the others. They rationalized that the Republicans were not responsible for atrocities to the same extent as the Fascists, since Republican violence was the work of ignorant Spanish peasants and workers, and Fascist atrocities were the handiwork of aristocrats. A friend, Denis Campkin, who had great scrupulousness in these matters, pointed out that while Spender and his friends grew indignant at the shelling of refugees from cities captured by Franco, they said nothing in protest to similar actions committed by the Republicans. Perhaps he was right, and Spender admits the speciousness of his own arguments. He is sure above all of only one thing: that one must be honest. Atrocities committed by Republicans must be admitted and protested. At this point, of course, he found himself on collision course with his Communist friends and colleagues.

But if indeed there were significant differences between the 1920s and the succeeding decade, nothing could be more different than the world of the 1930s (the period of intervention and non-intervention) from that of the rising 1940s. The 1930s heard the last gasp of the expiring idea that the individual, accepting his responsibilities, could alter the history of his time. From that point on, the individual could only conform to or protest against forces and events which were beyond his personal control.

Thus the 1930s which seemed so revolutionary, were in reality the end of the liberal phase of history. Liberal individualists had their last chance to attach their ideals of democracy to a people's cause, the cause of Spanish republicanism. After that relatively small conflict, the total armament of the civilized world drowned all individual efforts in a rising flood of mechanized power. In other words, the characteristic of the 1930s was that a few people—of whom the members of the International Brigade were the outstanding examples—were aware of an encroaching domination of the world by power politics, amid the blindness of the majority. On the other hand, in the 1940s most people were aware of the situation; within the many were the few who recognized their almost complete lack of power. "The tragedy of the 1930's was the blindness of the many; the tragedy of the 1940's was the ineffectiveness of the few." [43]

The gravest weakness of the writers of what Spender called the pink decade or the divided generation was that they were "time-bound." They had made a wager that a world order of peace and social justice would emerge in their time, just as Wordsworth, Coleridge and Shelley had done in their day. And they lost, just as the Romantics had done, and were forced to spend their next phase searching for an attitude which would be independent of external events. The external event for Spender's generation was the German-Soviet Nonaggression Pact, the non-bomb which fell on liberalism.

So deep was the resulting disillusionment that it might almost have become a death wish: *Vienna* had shown a world which was not only sick but moribund. *Returning to Vienna* made a significant equation between the permanent sickness of the city and the temporary illness of the poet. In *The Trial of a Judge*, the Judge's wife indulges in what can only be called a paean to death. The Judge himself recognizes that his city is a place where death is so highly esteemed that the administrators of death are the political rulers of the nation (cf. Camus, *State of Siege*).

"The Dead Island" tightens the connection between the sickness of a city and the sickness of the hero, although it runs it in reverse: the hero is sick and thus reveals the world's illness. Dr. Rooth writes a letter of explanation concerning his male protégé and lover: " 'his behaviour expresses an intuition of a destructive spirit which really exists in the world in which we live.' " [44]

Another way of expressing this same truth is to say that

the protégé is the world. "In him is incarnated the moment when a civilization really begins to lose grip, when violence becomes an end in itself, history rushes, the boundaries of nations alter so rapidly that there is an inflation in the printing of maps, the bristling turreted forms of Gothic cathedrals suddenly live again in the swirling forms of battleships with their cargo of destruction and hell copied from the nightmares of mediaeval artists." [45]

If the protégé's spirit is destructive how can he be considered a creative artist? "Where there is tyranny and fear, nothing is created. How, then, shall one condemn an artist who, being unable to create, lives in his own being, the poem, the dance, the madness, which he apprehends from the world around him? The difference between art and madness or intoxication is this: the artist projects and re-creates outside himself a world of ideas which he puts in order: the madman or the inebriate *is* a world of disordered ideas." [46]

The hero of the novella "The Burning Cactus" says furiously that his life is like dry, bitter, cutting cactus. So, self-destructively, playfully but without humor, he sets fire to a plant, the wind blows, branches of fire spring along the grass to other cacti, the whole hillside (the world) is aflame and the human beings who caused it all must run for their lives. If this is linked to Werner's impassioned initiation of Tom in "The Cousins" we see the careless human criminals, idly and yet angrily setting fire to the world. Werner hates the memory of the first conflagration in 1914; he feels powerless to prevent a second. So all the disillusioned liberal can do is to warn the charming young denizen of a great English country house that "while you were still thinking about games . . . while you were nestling in the world composed of the summer, Eton, this old house, you would be simply pitchforked into the war like so much hay standing in those fields and soon to be cut down." [47]

As *World Within World* made abundantly clear, Stephen Spender has always been concerned, under one philosophy or another, with the problem of the proper relationship of the individual to the group. An early poem about juvenile experience suggests this problem by its very title: "My Par-

ents Kept Me from Children Who Were Rough" (*Poems*).
They were rough indeed, and the small boy feared them.
They copied his lisp behind his back; they jumped out of
hedges to frighten him; they threw mud while the boy pre-
tended to smile. But he did not hate them; he admired
them immensely and above all else would have liked to be
accepted by them—he longed to forgive them, but they
never smiled in return. The echo of this poem about the
poet's childhood reverberates through the seemingly innocent bit of dialogue when Mrs. Brand is taking Geoffrey to
the station to join a group of boys returning to Tisselthorp:
"Mrs. Brand looked at the boys and smiled quite gaily.
'Well, they all look happy and friendly,' she said to the
headmaster, their mothers, and partly even to them themselves. 'I'm sure they're not rough.' 'Mummy!' The word
hung on the ears of the silently perceptive little chorus." [48]
And on their memories, no doubt, just as the alienating-
attractive word *rough* hung on the poet's memory.

When the young poet, the "Rupert Brooke of the De-
pression," was troubled by widespread unemployment, he
felt guilty because he was a member of the exploiting class,
and powerless to join the working class. In Germany he met
an unemployed young man whom he calls Jimmy Younger
in *World Within World*. He took him in and the narrative
seems to indicate that Younger became his servant, companion, friend, and lover. Although Spender speaks often of his
desire to identify himself with some other male, in actual
fact, it was Younger who had to adjust to Spender's friends,
his way of life, travel schedule, personal likes and dislikes.
This then led Spender paradoxically but nevertheless actually to despise Younger as an empty person with no life of
his own.

Just previous to meeting Younger, Spender and Christopher Isherwood had been in Berlin. There Isherwood knew
everybody and had a rich fabric of connections into which
to introduce Spender. So Spender played the Younger role.
But when Isherwood returned to London, he discovered to
his chagrin, both that Spender had been indiscreet in barking Isherwood's personal anecdotes all over London, but

that he was a bit of a literary lion in his own right and therefore his life could no longer revolve in orbit, with such naïve simplicity, about Isherwood's sun. Younger, Spender, and Isherwood had clearly "come against the difficulty which confronts two men who endeavour to set up house together. Because they are of the same sex, they arrive at a point where they know everything about each other and it therefore seems impossible for the relationship to develop beyond this. . . . loyalty demanded, since the relationship itself could not develop, that neither of us should develop his own individuality in a way that excluded the other. Thus a kind of sterility was the result of the loyalty of each to the other; or rather of his loyalty to the relationship itself which he did not wish to grow beyond." [49] One wonders if Spender were not simply describing the impasse in heterosexual relationships well known as domesticity—that point in marital relationship at which surprises or new discoveries no longer seem possible?

And what if these two companions are intellectual equals who share common interests? "A relationship with an intellectual equal would have been even more open to the same objection. For the differences of class and interest between Jimmy and me certainly did provide some element of mystery which corresponded almost to a difference of sex." [50]

A great deal of this argument seems the most arrant nonsense because it would preclude not only homosexual relationship but heterosexual as well. The idea that because two persons are of the same sex they automatically have perfect understanding of each other is so puerile as to be immediately discarded as serious argument. Place against this homosexual analysis Chaucer's well-known studies in the *Canterbury Tales* of the struggles within marriage concerning which shall have the sovereignty, husband or wife. One might advance the suggestion that what Spender called identifying himself completely with another person was actually a subtle form of aggression.

Spender follows these passages with a more careful consideration of the topic. "Love for a friend expressed a need for self-identification. Love for a woman, the need for a relationship with someone different, indeed opposite, to myself." [51] Spender added the provisos however, that self-identification leads to frustration if it is not realized at all; to destruction, perhaps, if it is half-realized; to sterility if it is realized completely. "The relationship of a man with the 'otherness' of a woman is a relationship of opposite poles. They complete, yet never become one another, never reach a static situation where everything which is possible to be known between two people is known, every gesture a repetition of one already performed, where little development, except the loss of youth, seems possible beyond this." [52] Here is Spender's absolute denial of the possibility of bored domesticity in marriage, despite the enormous bulk of evidence to the contrary.

"How Strangely This Sun Reminds Me of My Love!" (*Poems*) refers to staring at the other male's face, taking his photograph on the retina of the memory on the very first morning of identification. But this concentration seems to result in the utter corruption of the other's sunlike confidence. So that even in the things Younger was formerly expert, such as the turning of bolts or the driving of machines, now his hand fumbles. This is the net result for the beloved. And for the poet? He has quite the best of it, for the sun returns the image of the beloved, the river his photograph, the ascending lark the ringing fulness of his voice.

A whole group of poems ("Love and Separation") in *Collected Poems* have to do with a girl whom the poet loved but who left him for another love. If it were not for Helen's constant misunderstanding of Meredith, one might call them a modern reworking of the acid, corrosive quality of Meredith's *Modern Love*. Thus heterosexual love turns out to have its peculiar demerits also.

Three poems represent a significant shift from private to public thinking. "An 'I' Can Never Be Great Man" (*Poems*) claims that the first person singular can no longer be central; now the one who would seek fame must sink his personal identity in the first person plural. In "Exiles from Their Land, History Their Domicile" (*The Still Centre*) the lonely poet desires solidarity with others who were exiles in their lives but are now gathered together on sacred shores. The Judge (*Trial of a Judge*) discovers that to know final reality in the midst of time is always to suffer exile from the land of the living. The drama portrays in strong rhetoric the predicament of liberal individualism caught between fascism and communism—impossible alternatives because either one would destroy the individual. "The Bombed Happiness" (*The Still Centre*) is a sad poem of initiation, in which the innocent child, not yet aware of his own identity, is forced by society into an acceptable role, thus making it impossible for him to ever know what he really is or could be. Spender's sonnet, "The World Wears Your Image on the Surface" (*The Still Centre*), explores the social myopia which judges the inside from a preconceived idea of the outside. But the poet plunges into the eye, bores into the inner self and permits himself to drown in the other life.

The frequently expressed desire of the poet to drown in some other life is poignantly expressed in "Variations on My Life—the Second" (*The Still Centre*). He is walking in the street or riding on a train. In the distance he sees a face full of promise. He takes the face down into the subterranean region of fantasy and endows it with all the qualities he most desires, but he is always dragged out again into the bleak day.

The collection of novella, *The Burning Cactus*, contains many references to the problem of the relationship of the individual to the group. When the heroine of "The Dead Island" hears about the intimate relationship of Dr. Rooth and her young lover, it hammers down her own isolation. Later she repentently recognizes that true knowledge of people does not see them in orbit about the self, but quite separate from the self, "running in their own grooves." [53] Finally she comes to recognize that only the dead have real community, because they are all "heaped together." [54] The living are explorers who live out their lives alone in vast arctic landscapes. In "The Cousins" Spender seems to see himself as Werner, and suffers the agony of guessing how odd and alien he looks to a young lad he particularly cares for. [55] Helen, also in "The Cousins," has never told her sons that they have partial Jewish ancestry because that might tend to set them apart from the other county gentry; on the other hand she has never told them about sex because she wants them to save their sexuality for the right time and the one person.[56] In the same novella, Werner wonders, as he abruptly leaves the country estate, which of them exist and which are the dead? They represent an old, dying way of life, but they are much more at home in their moribund world than he is in his creative world, so the total impact was "ghostly." [57]

An old and dying way of life can still manage, even in its moribund state, to separate children and to give superiority for entirely wrong reasons: " 'We will proceed with the inquisition,' said Palmer" in *The Backward Son*. " 'Brand, what *class* is your father?' 'How do you mean, what class?' asked Geoffrey, frightened either to speak or not to speak. 'My father keeps a newspaper shop,' said Palmer, 'so he's middle class. Laughton's father's a doctor, so he's higher middle class. The fat yellow-eyed daughter of a bitch who spawned the toad known to long-suffering humanity as Fallow, is a washerwoman, isn't she, Fallow? So he's lower class.' A howl of misery was the reply. 'Shut up, or—' said Palmer, suddenly sitting bolt upright in bed, in a voice that was still quieter, still more penetrating. There was silence. 'Now, Brand, answer my question.' 'My father is an M.P., and he knows several Lords. I think we must be First Class,' answered Geoffrey, with a thrill of pride. All the sons of tradesmen, even Palmer, were silent. Then Palmer said: 'All right. Good night. Night all.' And they all rolled over on their sides and went to sleep." [58]

Perhaps beneath all his disappointment with the world, lay Spender's recognition of a death wish both in the world and in himself, a sense of bankrupt liberalism and of the sure immediate victory of fascism, canceled out only eventually by the final victory of communism. Perhaps behind his attempts to use contemporary idiom in his poems and his fretful anxiety about whether an upper-class poet could ever be accepted by the working class, lay the deeper malaise, How would I fit in any group? This question could be answered by saying I am superior, but although the poet does often feel superior, this is not a *modus vivendi* which makes it possible for him to live comfortably in the world. Generally he has a nagging feeling of envy for people who, although they may not be superior in intellect or talent are clearly superior in their ability to manage the outside world with comfort and efficiency. He attempts to drown himself in another individual and the struggle for dominance inevitably begins; he attempts to merge his life in a classless society and his liberal individualism makes him a conspicuous misfit. Perhaps Mrs. Brand's smiling optimism is the real goal of his life: " 'Well, they all look happy and friendly.' " All to be happy and friendly, individuality preserved and relationship both established and maintained.

3

Louis MacNeice: The Circular Movement

After co-editing the annual undergraduate anthology, *Oxford Poetry: 1929*, with Stephen Spender, Louis MacNeice published his first collection of poems, *Blind Fireworks*, in 1929. Like Chinese fireworks, the poems go through their light random popping antics against the somber background of secular holiday or religious festival, then fall and go out.[1] Quite expectedly, many poems are about childhood experience: the pleasures and dangers of sleep, reminiscences of life in rectory and church, and many references to classical deities. But even so early a collection grants two glimpses of social concern. In the foreword MacNeice charmingly expresses his admiration for the Chinese because they invented gunpowder not to kill people, but to entertain them with fireworks. He links the "Time-God" Thor with the "Man-of-Science" Pythagoras by having them both serve as figures for the passage of time. But the selections make clear that something more is meant than the ordinary passage of time. This is the final or end-time which theology calls eschatology—a theme of doom introduced early (1929) and coming to maturity in the radio-drama *Out of the Picture* (1938).

"This Tournament" evokes the delicate imagery of moths jousting in the sun, smashed by the descending hammer of Thor. Even Pythagoras, who explains and supports the universe mathematically, is warned, in "A Lame Idyll," that his own era is coming to an end and that he too will fall into the dustheap along with Adonis and Proserpine. The dead gods circle about the contemporary symbol of an industrial chimney in "Twilight of the Gods." The abacus of Pythagoras is broken; he can no longer keep the world steady by counting. "Coal and Fire" is topically concerned with the industrial revolution, but thematically points to a revolution in which the "damned" middle and the golden mean will find no place at all. "Adam's Legacy" contains only two possible choices: stand before a door that will not open, or quietly await the trump of doom.

"The Court Historian (A Satirical Composition)" metes to the scholar the same short shrift MacNeice had already given to Pythagoras. The historian sits godlike, inscribing the dates of dynasties, oblivious to a figure about to tap him on the shoulder and usher him into past history. "Candle Poems" innocently describe shrinking cylinders standing in increasing islands of wax. But a breakwater of wax is inadequate protection for an island against the tides of a troubled time. Candles are more appropriate to the foot of a single casket, or to the demise of a total culture. This theme of dying culture is further developed in "Neurotics" as the poet compares Aeneas fleeing successfully from burning Troy with modern man who is destined to perish along with his moribund culture.

Roundabout Way (1932), a novel, contains such scenes of social criticism as when Janet quite literally breaks free from the Victorian era by smashing an enormous dining-room mirror with a decanter of port! Because of his frantic fear of bolshevism, Sir Randal establishes an international youth movement and uses as his figurehead, the Reverend John Bilbatrox: "filthy vulture-face, fleshy and pouched and foul, selfish and sensual, pig-pike and serpent." Hegley, the representative of the academic profession, is essentially cold and anticreative. He is a born critic because of a constitutional inability to be vulgar or crude.

T. S. Eliot published MacNeice's first volume of verse after Oxford. *Poems* (1935) is insistently contemporary with an emphasis upon wireless, factory chimneys, policemen, and buses fulfilling Michael Roberts's prescription: "It was inevitable that the growth of industrialism should give rise to a 'difficult' poetry . . . abrupt, discordant, intellectual."

But if the circumference of MacNeice's language and imagery is determinedly social, the center is warmed by personal characterization. And whereas for many proletarian poets the singing voice grows strident and the intellectual tone doctrinaire, MacNeice was saved by the coolness and virtuosity of his performance. The complex meanings and the large issues tend to be expressed in delightful doggerel with childlike naïveté. The result is a cool distancing of sentiment and doctrine that makes both palatable.

Poems begins with "An Eclogue for Christmas," a form much favored by MacNeice, the dialogue precursor of his later verse plays. *A* is the urban half of a personality which is *B* in the country. His world is so full of nonessential sweets that it might be called a "diabetic" culture. Drums and Hawaiian guitars drown the cry for identity. Like modern art, his life has been splintered and abstracted; symbol, or pastiche, but is never just itself. Full of liabilities, with no assets, there is hope of no new beginning; there is only the certainty of an end when the "Goths" will again "come swarming down the hill." Flats, clubs, beauty parlors—all the trivia of contemporary culture, will be mowed down by young men with machine guns.

B, the rural side of the modern personality, is a grim Hardy protagonist rather than a hearty Fielding squire. Every place is simply a spot to die. The county gentry have declined into male alcoholics and tweedy women who still attempt to hunt and farm although factory smoke pollutes the air and settles down on field and forest. Eventually all these private manors will be socialized, and the survivors of the gentry will be talented buffoons or prostitutes. The countryside evokes only memories of the past and the wisdom of nonassertive animals and stones. So from his rural attempt at escape, *AB* must return to London, to be anesthetized by saxophones, xylophones, canvases in galleries, canvas sails on rich men's yachts, and the final technical perfection of a grilled steak.

Culture is in decline; escape is impossible; modern life is intrinsically trivial; and the hopeless truths may be made only grimly acceptable by witty statement. There is much use of rhyme to make the poetry sound childishly singsong and somehow parodic. The vocabulary is more frequently the words for material things than for philosophic concepts. The total effect is an adult critique of what is wrong with England and a Stoic courage in the face of despair.

The substitution of things for theories is noticeable in "Train for Dublin" when the poet toasts "incidental" things rather than symbolic images of painted wood. The search for meanings is abandoned for the simple experience of each thing "exactly" as it is. The eschatological vision of *Blind Fireworks* is continued and amplified in *Poems*. In "Morning Sun," the radiant splashing of the fountain in the square is quickly transformed to dust-grey powder. In "Persons," the Greek hero swings the Gorgon's head wide, everything living is turned to stony death and an empty earth spins like a mad moth around a blackening sun.

"To a Communist" is an antidoctrinaire toast. Before the Party member preens himself on his dialectical solution to all society's ills, he should remember that the snow which purifies everything overnight may also melt in a single day. "The Wolves" is a sad and hopeless warning of danger. The enemies of freedom howl about England's coast. All that the liberal and conservative politicians can think of is to form a circle and join hands, or to build ineffective little sand castles on the beach, temporarily blotting out the howls with talk and laughter. In "Aubade," the poet remembers the dreams of youth when he assumed that the unnecessary mythologizing of life would end in an enlightened *Götterdämmerung* and the consequent exaltation of humanity. But now in maturity he sees only the stark light of early dawn falling on urban brick facades, and hears only the voices of newsboys announcing war. "Spring Voices" warns the suburbanite that even while he putters about in the garden, gambles on horses, or buys cigars, he may "loiter into a suddenly howling crater" or fall over backward "garrotted by the sun." Using the imagery of a circus, MacNeice barks that laboring men are no longer obedient; respectability has come to an end; we live on sufferance awaiting disaster. The world is a trapeze with the ropes wearing thin, and we all know that circus jobs, sooner or later, spell death.

The last poem in the volume, "Ode," preserves Mac-Neice's wishes for his infant son. Unlike himself, he should not have any great love for the infinite or the absolute. Let him have five good senses instead. Ominous images threaten his little life: a fly on the windowpane, tulips in a hearse, a cock crowing in the dark, and an airplane in a June sky. The vaguely ominous becomes more precise as the poet transforms the buzzing fly into a roaring plane, with its promise of war and death.

In 1937 Louis MacNeice wrote a radio drama, *Out of the Picture*, for which his earlier eclogues and serenades might have been technical preparation. The decision to write for a new popular medium was in itself significant democratization of the Oxford poet. In his introduction to a later radio play (*Christopher Columbus* [1944]),[2] MacNeice thought about the techniques of verse drama which is broadcast. In consideration of the quick boredom of a radio audience, accustomed to bad art, the unconsciousness of itself as a cooperating audience, the scholarly MacNeice suggests forgetting about literature and concentrating on sound! For literature began as sound with the Homeric singers or the Icelandic skalds shouting over the zoolike noises of crude banquets. Tankards clashed, babies bawled, fires smoked, and old men snored and snuffled in their sleep. Poetry is the most primitive form of literature and therefore especially designed for this kind of audience. A printed page of poems may frighten away an average man; the rhythmic appeal of the radio to the ear alone may not strike him as verse at all. However, MacNeice recommended that the radio writer must use brief time spans, move faster in leading to climax, avoid confusing the listener with sideshows and irrelevancies, and choose actors who sound more like people than thespians.

Out of the Picture repeats the ominous suggestion of *Poems* with the warning of the Radio Announcer, early in the play, that slapstick can easily turn to swordplay, cottage flowers may hiss like snakes, and familiar trees suddenly deliver a *coup de grâce* on the nape of the neck. The setting of the play is a world which faces final annihilation in war. The persons in charge of the moribund world are bailiffs, psychiatrists, ministers of peace who function as directors of war, and movie actresses; in other words, legalists, specialists in lunacy, and venal politicians as the chief representatives of a corrupt popular culture.

The hero of the play, Portright, is a bad artist who prides himself on his nonpolitical nature, exults in his defeatism and lostness, and finally, at the end of the play, emerges momentarily into the political world by shooting the minister of peace. His girl friend, Moll, and a charwoman are the hopes of the world because they have maintained physical health, animal instincts, and human sympathy. Moll must kill Portright because his neuroses will not be able to bear the consequences of his heroic assassination. So, quietly and lovingly she slips poison into his cup of celebration.

It is an offstage chorus that chants the eschatological meaning of the play: the golden cycle is ended; Troy, Babylon, and Nineveh are consumed by fire—London will be next. It is the individual modern man who has been pushed "out of the picture" by the pressure of mass-man bombs, and gas. When Moll pronounces her rather moving benediction: " 'I will give you sons. Good luck go with them,' " it is clear that only the emotions are assuaged and only luck is invoked. The reason knows precisely what chance mere biological continuity has in the face of foreordained doom.

One unfortunate consequence of dealing, not with absolutes and infinities, but with unique individuals is the problem of multitudinousness. As the London *Times* commented, the weakness of the play "lies not in dealing in abstractions, but in trying to crowd in far more concrete and present matters than even so loose a form can hold and remain a form." [3] Yet the multiplicity of effects to which the critic objected may be the strong intention of the playwright. The constant interruptions of announcer, chorus, auctioneer, singers, and peace-conference news may be essential to show modern man deluged by noise, lost in crowds, and continually plucked at by the opinion-molders.

The play moves with rapid pace, leaping intermittently from comedy to tragedy, and the hopelessness of its ending is made all the stronger because the playwright did not weep all through the beginning.

Louis MacNeice indicated his membership in a group of working poets by publishing a strange travel book, *Letters from Iceland,* in 1937, written in collaboration with W. H. Auden. The former was aware of the dangers of literary co-operation with so strong a personality and laughingly confessed that Day-Lewis wrote worst when he attempted a slapdash Audenesque satire, whereas MacNeice suffered most when he forced himself to feel things that he actually merely thought: "feelings are one's own, but thoughts come from the group." [4]

Auden was drawn to Iceland by his Scandinavian ancestry and an interest in the Norse saga. Under contract to Faber and Faber to do a travel book, he arrived in Iceland first and was later joined by MacNeice and other friends. Lest they brood over the *ultima Thule* of the ancient world, he brought along a breezy satirical volume by Lord Byron. Five chapters of the travel book (1, 5, 8, 13, 16) become the racy installments of a *terza rima* letter from the twentieth-century British poets isolated at the world's end to the nineteenth-century Romantic poet exiled in Greece. The chapters illustrate Auden's remarkable ability to parody anyone from Skelton through Tennyson to Kipling, as he conveys brilliant insights and scrupulous trivia with the well-known lighthearted, casual touch. MacNeice points out that "Byron's lighter stanzas . . . are a . . . more elastic form, able to carry the discursive comments of a Don Juan on a world of flux and contradictions." As for his companion and co-author, Auden "holds strongly that chat belongs to poetry as well as incantation or lyrical statement, uses it easily and lucidly to give with point and humor a memorable summary of his position." [5] Auden had actually considered the possibility of addressing their verse epistles to Jane Austen, of all unlikely people, but the grim little spinster frightened him on two fronts: the novel he considered to be "a higher art than poetry altogether"; and the middle-class, unmarried virgin had altogether too sharp an understanding of the "economic basis of society." [6]

The book is quite self-consciously a collage: photographs, press clippings, statistics, graphs, gossip, natural scenery, men and women, the arts, the European news—and, above all else, Auden and MacNeice themselves. By far the best things in the book, besides the Byron letter, are the "Last Will and Testament" of both poets, and the "Eclogue from Iceland" and the "Epilogue" by MacNeice alone. "Last Will and Testament" (chapter 17), which begins with family concerns, moves in stanza 32 to the public world as the beneficiaries become as current as the items on page one of the local press. Stanley Baldwin, who obviously needs a new facade, is bequeathed the false front of Lincoln Cathedral; Ramsay MacDonald, with his talent for sudsy sentimentality, receives the Cheshire soapworks; Frank Buchman, the founder of the Moral Re-Armament Movement (formerly called the Oxford Group), is given his pick of one hundred converts from the social register. Because he so obviously needs it, a little Christian joy goes to gloomy Dean Inge; because his dogmatic precision needs exposure to the common life, I. A. Richards is given a stay in an English boarding house; and since nothing could embarrass him more, Bertrand Russell is bequeathed a belief in God. Then the brilliant journalistic contemporaneity moves into the little coterie of Oxford and London friends, their private peccadilloes, and their very private personal jokes.

The "Eclogue from Iceland" (chapter 10), consists of a conversation on the Arnarvatn Heath between Craven (presumably Auden), Ryan (MacNeice), the ghost of Grettir (hero of one of the last of the Icelandic sagas), and the Voice of Europe. Grettir asks if Craven and Ryan are also islanders, where "the Lowest Common labels" are put on everything. Ryan replies that on his island (Ireland) his compatriots shoot "straight in the cause of crooked thinking." Craven points out that they are all three exiles: Grettir sentenced to eternal wandering by the curse of a foe; Craven in Spain at Easter time, running away from his own household gods with no intention of finding new gods. Now,

in Iceland, he and Ryan are simply exploring more of the
surface of men's lives and coming up with bright, journalistic copy. Grettir urges Ryan and Craven to go back where
they came from. It is their clear duty; it may also be their
last chance. When Ryan considers the London to which
they will return, the long catalogues of the modern malaise
are handled with superlative ease. The Voice of Europe, full
of self-pity, death wish, and self-indulgence, will sing its
universal anodyne, but Ryan thanks God for those who dare
to go their own way, who do not kiss "the arse of law and
order," or purchase comfort at the price of pride.

There is a curious irony involved in the climactic advice
of Grettir to return to their own land to make their personal
witness for individual freedom. In "Valediction" (*Poems*
[1935]), the youthful MacNeice had vowed to exorcise Ireland from his blood. Now the two young intellectuals are
being counseled by a heroic voice from a past they themselves have condemned and fled. But the response of Mac-
Neice to the advice of his own poem is disillusioning to say
the least. Grettir claimed that he might have fled to the
anonymity of the Orkney Islands or the Hebrides. Although
MacNeice agreed with the Auden dictum that traveling
deals only with surfaces and news copy, yet the very next
year, 1937, MacNeice is found in the very islands, the Hebrides, to which Grettir was too proud and resolute to flee.

Back in Hampstead Heath, in a book-lined room, Louis
MacNeice writes an "Epilogue for W. H. Auden" to rehearse the Icelandic trip before the memory slips away.
While their pleasant holiday contained no great happenings
at all, the world had been putting on a "graver show":
Seville fell in southwest Spain, the Olympic games were
held and Hitler spouted Aryan nonsense. In his apartment,
MacNeice waits for a telephone to ring. The cushions, rugs,
and creature comforts there are only a thin disguise over a
veritable desert, and the silent telephone a mockery of the
need for human comradeship. If Auden were there, they
would drink coffee and tell tales, aware that their "pre-
rogatives as men" could be canceled at any moment. He
lifts the poetic-toast, aware that before the poem can be

read, a "gun-butt" might rap upon the door. In a sense, the bachelor apartment at Hampstead and the boiling sulphur basins in Iceland are both eschatological evidences. They look pleasant, domestic, harmless; but they signify the vale of Armageddon on Judgment Day.

Nineteen thirty-eight was Louis MacNeice's *annus mirabilis* in which he had four volumes published: *I Crossed the Minch*, another travel book; *Zoo*, chatty comment on animals and people; *The Earth Compels*, a volume of poetry; and *Modern Poetry*, prose criticism of modern poetry. Because MacNeice knew no Gaelic and the Hebrideans spoke nothing else, *I Crossed the Minch* was condemned to be "a tripper's book written by someone who was disappointed and tantalized by the islands and seduced by them only to be reminded that on the soil he will always be an outsider." [7] He might have taken tart comfort from the acid remark of Samuel Johnson who classified Gaelic, in 1773, as "the rude speech of a barbarous people, who had few thoughts to express and were content, as they conceived grossly, to be grossly understood."

MacNeice chose to go to the Hebrides for a reason analogous to Auden's decision to go to Iceland; he hoped the Celt in him would be drawn out by a primitive culture which went deep into his forbears. But oddly he was unprepared for the wholesale emigration from the islands, a phenomenon that Dr. Johnson had noted in the eighteenth century. He was also sadly disappointed to discover that instead of insularity guaranteeing the continuity of the primitive culture, the islands were themselves the victims of cultural invasion from the mainland. The primitive culture was dead; the engrafted culture had not yet taken firm root: "More than one generation is required before a man can be a capitalist with grace." [8]

In a very controversial section about the effect of the Soviet Union upon indigenous cultures, MacNeice accepts the often-repeated praise that the Soviets maintained local traditions and cultures wherever possible, although always within the framework of subservience to the new order. This pattern appeals to MacNeice as the ideal way to link conservation of the old with radical zeal for the adventurous new. But instead of producing this rich cultural brew, it seems to him that his left-wing comrades in England "suffer from the masochism of the puritan." Instead of personal enrichment, party membership permits no frills, comforts, or luxuries for the body or the mind. Individual persons and unique communities must be liquidated for the sake of economic cooperation and the united statement of the Marxist creed. To MacNeice so bleak a social philosophy looks like a "future of Esperanto, Sunday School treats and homage to the Highest Common Factor" (cf. "Eclogue from Iceland").[9] But again he reminds himself that Lenin recognized the necessary role of differentiation, and at this point, in the margin of my copy, a previous reader wrote "Poor Fish."

In an important and topical, but also whimsical interview with his Guardian Angel, MacNeice is asked if he has read *Forward from Liberalism*, that "nice" book by his friend Stephen Spender. Besides, isn't it about time he took some definite position on political issues? The divided poet replies that his sympathies are leftist, both intellectually and spiritually. "I would vote Left any day, sign manifestos, answer questionnaires. . . . My soul is all for moving towards the classless society." But so far as heart and "gut" are concerned, "man for me is still largely characterized by what he buys. . . . I am both a money snob and a class snob." Even in his attitude toward women, MacNeice likes them better if they are rich and perhaps have "Honourable" before their names. He especially values the gestures, poise, and intonations which are "imitated from snobs by a snob and practiced for the seduction of snobs." This dividedness is not a tension to be released, but a sign that the poet is irrevocably one of the lost intelligentsia. Thus, to the precise and probing penultimate speech of the Guardian Angel: "Are you going to, partly out of pique, partly out of vanity, but mainly because you are just darn bone lazy, wilfully espouse a life of outmoded triviality and inaction—" the poet who is weary of fighting and always losing the same battles can only mutter "Oh, go to hell."[10]

"Bagpipe Music" swishes its kilts and skirls its tune but

ends with the same ominous peal of doom. In this fast-moving, slangy bit of cynicism, modern man is seen to care nothing for Eastern spiritual disciplines or new world religions, but he manages to get by with a bank balance and "a bit of skirt in a taxi." The last quatrain brilliantly combines the dapper patter with an ominous warning:

It's no go my honey love, it's no go my poppet;
Work your hands from day to day, the winds will blow the
    profit.
The glass is falling hour by hour, the glass will fall for ever.
But if you break the bloody glass you won't hold up the
    weather.[11]

The last poem in *I Crossed the Minch*, "On Those Islands (A Poem for Hector MacIver)," observes that the old culture survives to some degree in the smaller fishing villages of the islands where no one hurries, fires are still built of peat, Gaelic tunes are preserved intact, and the parlor photographs of island sons who were successful in the New World strike the only discordant modern note. But this kind of simple peace, made by blotting out the modern world and remaining resolutely in the past, is "not for me," [12] says the poet, and implies probably not for anyone for very much longer.

Quite naturally, *Zoo* makes no extended comment on the human condition. But it strikes a few significant notes which ought not to be lost out of the total MacNeice harmony. As part of his usual critique of the labor dilemma of working men, he points out that for ninety percent of the people, their weekly tasks are unpleasant and boring: it is only on weekends that they come alive to express themselves, and then some two million of them visit the London Zoo.

On a bank holiday visit to Paris, MacNeice went to see the Zoo there. He discovered that its album opens with a quotation from André Demaison: "Lorsque dans les parcs modèles, les bêtes, même privées de leur climat d'origine, sont entourées de confort, de soins, lorsqu'elles sont comprises dans leur conscience profonde, elles arrivent à préférer cette paix, cette sécurité, aux errances et aux terreurs militaires." [13] The English poet wants to ask the French writer how he knows that the animals prefer the security of captivity to the dangers of freedom. And even if they do, ought they to be encouraged in such a preference? Then, in a delightful parody of the style and rhythm of Tennyson's "Locksley Hall," he recommends blood, hunger, and fear of the dark as being a more healthful and natural state than all the comforts of a prison with the certainty of buns. At this point the cross-channel argument begins to sound like the dialogue between John the Savage and Moustapha Mond in Aldous Huxley's *Brave New World.* Or as Mac-Neice puts it: "Original Sin won for us a life of progress, pattern of dark and light, the necessity of winning our bread which builds our wits, the tension without which there is no music and the conflict without which there is no harmony." [14]

The Earth Compels, a volume of poems published by Faber and Faber in London in 1938, contains very little new work, and the new poems largely deal with older themes. "Homage to Clichés," one of MacNeice's best poems, is both complex in structure and subtle in transformation of image. "Sometimes, more fantastically, I take several images and ring the changes on them. Thus in a philosophical poem 'Homage to Clichés,' I think of the brute Other, the fate which we cannot influence: (a) as an Egyptian Rameses, (b) as a tenor bell (which we cannot peal but can only play chimes upon), (c) as a black panther (black because unknown and because the black panther is popularly said to be untamable). The movement of each of these three will be the movement of Fate." [15]

"Homage to Clichés" embodies MacNeice's favorite game of the ominous clue lurking in the banal social situation. How pleasant to sit in a bar with an attractive woman and make the kind of conversation that requires no effort and no thought. But through a hidden door, up a belfry stair, hang eight black bells within a womb of stone. We imagined that our manipulation of them as chimes was the only sound they could make. But ringers are removing their coats to toll rather than to chime, and a timekeeper with watch and pistol stands ready to signal the end of the whole delightful world of cliché and refrain.

"Hidden Ice" is a complex poem which begins bravely to praise the heroes of domestic life, the routine workers who spend their lives being faithful to trivial tasks. But not all achieve this quiet heroism; some strike hidden ice. MacNeice was often told that this poem was obscure in meaning because of its condensation of language, therefore he took the trouble to explicate it. The ones who fall away from their loyal allegiance "are persons who become unable to keep their aesthetic sense or their outside interests or their erotic emotions pigeon-holed off into the hours when they are not on duty. They become obsessed by something which, on their system, should not be allowed to intrude into their eight-hour day. They kiss flowers and [become] like Judas because the act is treacherous to their whole system." Mac-Neice offers the example of a routine worker who becomes an active Communist: "And some of these people become fatally addicted to what belongs, on their premises, to their pet hours only. Such people in everyday life may end in suicide or the asylum. Such a man is like Saint Sebastian because his collapse is brought about through the things he loved—the arrow in his body feathered from the birds which he himself reared." [16]

Modern Poetry: A Personal Essay (1938) represents Louis MacNeice's most important body of literary criticism. The very first sentence of the preface binds the poet to the world: "This book is a plea for *impure* poetry, that is, for poetry conditioned by the poet's life and the world around him." As entertainer, the poet is tempted to fall over into escape literature; as critic, he may become so deeply committed to a particular school of thought that his verse becomes propaganda. The middle course is preferable not because it is the echo in verse of the prose convictions of the community, but because it becomes "its conscience, its critical faculty, its generous instinct." Ideological organizations will press him to "tell lies to order," but his job is to serve up poetic truth.

MacNeice muses that although his generation was profoundly influenced by Eliot and Pound while they were in school, they have turned instead to the writing of popular poetry—not popular because more people read it, but because it deals with man as a political animal with strong physical instincts, needs, and affections. Therefore the poetry of W. H. Auden, Stephen Spender, C. Day-Lewis, John Lehmann, Julian Bell, and William Plomer often deals with the economic, material, social, and sexual factors that are part of the lives of all modern men. They accept Marx and Freud, with their dialectics of materialistic socialism and the deep role of the physical instincts, as the chief architects of the modern mind. A secondary influence of Marx is the predilection for a world of concrete things rather than a shadowy universe of Platonic forms or Shelleyan ideas. Thus, forsaking the rebellion of the Romantics, the obscurity of the new metaphysicals, poets have now shifted back from withdrawal to involvement in the common life of men.

The poet is not different from other men, "he merely has more highly developed muscles and better coordination. And he practises his activity according to a stricter set of rules." Having restored the poet to normality, he performs the same office for the reader of poetry: "an ideal normal man who is an educated member of his own community and is basically at one with the poet in his attitude to life." [17]

Both of these definitions lead to the famous definition which has aroused the extremes of admiration or castigation: "I would have a poet able-bodied, fond of talking, a reader of newspapers, capable of pity and laughter, informed in economics, appreciative of women, involved in personal relationships, actively interested in politics, susceptible to physical impressions." [18] Thus *Modern Poetry* begins with the subtitle "A Personal Essay," and ends with the definition of the poet that fits no poet more aptly than it fits the author, Louis MacNeice.

In 1931 the Japanese invaded Manchuria, instigating an undeclared war which nibbled away implacably at China, and in 1937 struck at Shanghai and Nanking. In less than six months three hundred thousand Chinese soldiers and three hundred thousand civilians died. But the conflict never engaged the attention of the West. However, when a group of professional soldiers rose against the foundering Republican government of Spain, curiosity became concern, and sympathy was immediately transformed into personal action. Liberals everywhere construed the situation thus: General Francisco Franco, aided by reactionary officers, the Fascist Falange, the monarchists, the aristocrats, the rich, and the large landlords, is attempting to overturn a liberal, enlightened, legally elected government. Thus the Spanish Civil War had international repercussions far out of proportion to the numbers involved and the national significance. To military strategists it demonstrated the *blitz* value of planes and tanks against civilian populations. To ideologues, it was Right versus Left, Fascist versus Communist. To American writers with social consciences, it was "Hemingway's War." Anyone who fought against Franco wore the impeccable badge of liberalism.

MacNeice conveniently provided the statistics of involvement of his friends and himself in this classic confrontation. Edward Upward, the early inspiration of Auden and Isherwood, asserted in 1940 that no practitioner of the arts had anything to say unless he were in active participation in the "Worker's Movement." He wrote a novel about a neurotic upper-class youth who after two hundred pages of *Weltschmerz* finally emerges from his melancholia and goes out to find a worker—and MacNeice remarks irrepressibly, "as if that would solve everything," Auden and Isherwood made their contribution to the international proletarian revolution by producing what MacNeice called a "bad play, *On the Frontier*." Stephen Spender lectured across England on the topic "The Artist and Society," in which he attempted to turn the white peace doves of Picasso into the Holy Spirit of international Marxism.

In MacNeice's review, "The Poet in England Today," [19] he frankly admits his conviction that the "balance of right" was with the pro-Communist government of Spain, rather than with the pro-Fascist rebels. But comparing I. A. Richards's Ivory Tower of complete severance of poetry from be-

lief with the Brazen Tower of political propaganda, Mac-
Neice insists that the poet need not choose either extreme;
they are both partial, and self-limiting. The poet should sing
about the whole life of total men, and his voice should not
be projected through a megaphone.

These comments make fairly clear the position of Louis
MacNeice both in regard to the Spanish Civil War and in
relation to the involvement of his friends. He has stated
that the "political-animal" aspect of man must be included
in poetry. Intellectually and spiritually he is convinced of
the essential rightness of the leftist position. But the poetic
task seems larger to him than social significance; he must
also sing about man as unique individual.

In his foreword to *Poems: 1925–1948*, Louis MacNeice
pronounced *Autumn Journal* to be "in a sense, a failure; it
fails in depth. . . . we shall not be capable of depth—of
tragedy or *great* poetry—until we have made sense of our
world." It is quite natural that a verse diary of the public
events and private meanings from August 1938 through
January 1939 would be so caught up in the rush of event
that the *Journal* would be all foreground and little background, although, with shadows aplenty.

Autumn Journal joins those other diverse and greater
works of art—Shakespeare's *Othello* and Eliot's *The Waste
Land*—which explore dilemmas without suggesting solutions, and therefore leave both artist and audience with a
certain frustration and sense of incompletion. When Julian
Symons dubbed the *Journal* "The Bourgeois's Progress." [20]
he was making contrast rather than comparison, for the
point of Bunyan's great picaresque wandering is that Christian was illuminated by a heavenly vision and reached his
goal. *Autumn Journal* begins with the generalized good
will of the liberal, records amazement and shock at the
political events of the period, and ends with a diffuse
restatement of that same good will, badly shaken by events
and already recognized by the poet to be ineffectual. That
MacNeice was aware of these shortcomings is made clear
by the inadequacy of his defense. Concerning the ephemeral
topicality of the *Journal*, in a note he simply reminded the

critics of the natural limitations of the genre: "In a journal or a personal letter a man writes what he feels at the moment." In the face of the demand for solution or resolution in a work of art, MacNeice could offer only a disclaimer of intent: "Nor am I attempting to offer what so many people now demand from poets—a final verdict or a balanced judgment. . . . I refuse to be 'objective' or cleancut at the cost of honesty."

Cantos 1 through 4 move from Hampshire to London, from the beginning of August to the end of summer. Then in canto 5, on a beautiful day, Hitler speaks over the radio, and the bloody frontier of Auden and Isherwood is no longer just the theme of a bad play; it is the current reality of Everyman's life. It is no use to take refuge in the prayer of Jesus "Let this cup pass from me." We helped to mix the brew and it is only fair that we should join in drinking the liquor. Irresistably, his mind wanders back to his trip to Spain the preceding Easter (canto 6). He came home and promptly forgot Spain; now Spain has come to him in England.

The newspapers are full of conferences which adjourn before settlement, ultimata delivered by both sides, and over all the mad soprano shriek of Hitler's voice on the wireless (cantos 7, 8). The crisis will be settled in panic, and the resulting international relief will be only self-deception. He returns to Birmingham where he came to teach the Classics eight years before with his first wife. Now he is both wifeless and thrust by the international crisis out of his ivory tower. But the crisis is postponed: Chamberlain has saved the skins of Free Europe at the expense of their souls and the Czechoslovak nation goes down the drain.

In October (canto 9) the poet is back in London, the prey of sad thoughts about classical history. The ancient Greeks played out their little drama of truth and humor between the "jealous heaven" of the irresponsible gods and the indifference of the "callous sea." But free speech ended on Lacedemonian pikes, and Athens became a wall-less university town. The great talk went on for another thousand years, but it was no longer the epics of heroes. When the professor of Greek sought to recall the great free citizens of Greece all that came to mind was late Hellas, with crooks, opportunists, fancy boys, splitters of hairs, demagogues, quacks—borne on the impatient backs of all those slaves!

The return to his teaching duties (canto 10) reminds him that British education initiated the pupil into normal life—and of course it was assumed that things would always be normal in the British Isles. He is haunted in canto 11 by the girl of canto 4. Then it is Tuesday, October 25, 1938 (canto 12), and the golden weather reminds the classical scholar of a Roman mob crying for bread and circuses and caring nothing about freedom.

Perhaps one of the difficulties of a British classical education is that the graduate is all general, with no particularities, whereas, says MacNeice, the man on the street tends to have particular items of information but no general conceptual frame in which to fit them. Unfortunately, an Oxford graduate is left with an incapacity to ever believe anything again. The next evening (canto 14), the poet goes down to Oxford to vote and to help drive voters to the polling places. He goes partly for the fun of reunion, but also partly because he is coming to realize that the parliamentary system is the only defense of the citizen of a free society against the legionnaire's eagles of militarism and the lictors' axes of fascism. Perfectionists wait forever in a London fog; it is necessary to make crosses and blanks on votes even for unideal candidates. Unfortunately the best people are the very ones least likely to make solidarity of cause, but they must line up now against the beast.

Canto 15 describes the frenetic activities into which a pleasure-loving people throw themselves in order to blot out the thought of war. The poet (canto 16) recognizes that intellectuals, like Yeats, may become too aware of the cross-currents of motivation to take any appropriate action. Yet Yeats's beloved Maude Gonne saw it all and was still capable of purposeful action. Sitting in the November sun (canto 17) the poet recalls that just as Aristotle claimed that the heart of drama was in action, so man-in-action is the essential and only existent man. Once men held convictions with blood, bone, and pulse (canto 18); now they simply juggle possibilities in the brain. December brings bad news of the revival of the ghetto for the Jew, the gagging of free speech in the German universities, the growth of concentration camps for the enemies of the state.

At last, in canto 19 he can think of the lady of cantos 4 and 11 with no passionate reaction of resentment. He hopes she is busy, wishes her luck, and thanks for the party. On a visit to the National Gallery (canto 20) the arrogant Old Masters seem to affront the tentative systems of values of the modern world. They had such confidence, and we ask only to be left alone. A week before Christmas the poet thinks about the luxury gifts brought by the Magi to the very child destined to totally devalue them. The herald angels sing on the street corners, but not to announce peace to the waiting world, only to cadge for small coins.

A man ought to be like a fire (canto 21), spent recklessly but giving a good return; burning silence into sound, laughing at the dark, jumping into blaze from a single spark to purge and warm the world. On December 19 and the first snowfall in London (canto 22) the poet plans a visit to France for the trivia of eating, drinking, and a sophisticated but casual woman. He will not remain in Paris; he will cross the Pyrenees into the "pain and pride" of Spain (canto 23). The planes from Majorca, "modern Valkyries," bomb the city, while the matter-of-fact faith and courage of the populace shame all those who would dissolve truth in niggling petty distinctions.

Canto 24 begins with an invocation to sleep. May the conflicting selves the poet finds within wake up from that sleep healed and united; may his former wife sleep serenely beyond the Atlantic. But his dream is interrupted by coward doubts. The New Year is ushered in by bombs as well as bells, and tomorrow he must make decisions that call for action. Later on he can audit all the old accounts; later on he can sit in the sunshine; later he can see the whole design from its ending.

Autumn Journal records an indecision, which although lucidly mirrored, is not therein resolved, and thus continues to haunt his later work. Besides being a skillful poet, MacNeice is a very honest man. Therefore he recognizes that the gentle hedonism which he met in rectory and school, the bequest of nineteenth-century altruism, is too delicate a plant to survive long in the coming clash of the classes. Loathing fascism, and clearly dissatisfied with things as they are in England, he still cannot quite go all the way to the Communist position. Because he was part of the old world order that provided the forcing-frame for fascism, he therefore shares its guilt. But he is kept from doing anything constructive about the political threat, first because he feels helpless before the vastness of the problem, and second because he is hopeless about building a better future.

Beneath all the technical brilliance of the twenty-four cantos of this extraordinarily sustained long poem, there lies a blunt question which receives a bald answer: What can my kind of person be expected to do, in this kind of a world, at this terrifying moment? The obvious fact that the *Journal* fails to make sense of the world and therefore resolve the particular problems raised makes the answer unavoidable: nothing. It is pleasant to be assured that the river he will cross will not be the Styx of death, nor the Lethe of forgetfulness, but the Rubicon of decision. When? Oh, tomorrow. All accounts will be audited *later;* the sun will shine *later;* the answer to the problem equation will come out at the *last.*

And so, as John Peale Bishop put it, the Anglo-Irish poet plays out that bathetic tragedy, "The Hamlet of L. MacNeice." [21] Every bit as irresolute as Shakespeare's prince, he assigns to his leading character in *Out of the Picture* the stabbing of a surrogate Mr. Polonius Chamberlain. He goes down to Oxford instead of to Wittenberg in order to commit a public act which will release his frozen will. He proposes to win an election, which is promptly lost. No nunnery for his Ophelia; it simply takes three cantos to erase her from his memory. The bloody frontier he had sniffed at in the play of friends, now takes focus beside his bed, but he is as helpless before it as Hamlet in the face of Fortinbras's troops. Both Louis MacNeice and Prince Hamlet are haunted by father-ghosts, by soldier-ghosts, and most of all, by the ghost of a kingdom's dead greatness.

The last week of March, Louis MacNeice completed a group of poems published later in 1940 by the Cuala Press, Dublin, Ireland, under the title *The Last Ditch*. It was an unpretentious printing of four hundred and fifty copies, and the dedicatory quatrain to Eleanor Clark is unpretentious, too: these poems are not "heroic," they lack the power that comes from coherent and passionate belief. The poet is "rich" technically and intellectually; he is "not rich" in terms of affirmation, confidence, and faith. The poems are slight "odds or ends." Among them the "thief" of contemporary history may be located bundled up "in the last ditch," an ex-liberal with his back against the wall of his self-imposed limitations.

"Prognosis" is an elegant literary ballad concerning the possibilities of the coming spring. After *Autumn Journal* the poet has both sharpened and wiped his pen in order to write lines which are witty with slant rhyme, and lyrical with restrained passion and sadness. A tea leaf in the cup heralds the arrival of a stranger. Will it be John the Baptist to herald a new Incarnation, or will it be the prophet Jonah to announce that in forty days the world will end?

There are sixteen poems which the author groups under "The Coming of War." Four of the group have Irish settings: "Dublin," "Cushendun," "Sligo and Mayo," and "Galway." Generally they draw the contrast between the idyllic landscape and the coming of war. The relics of the past tell a story of ancient wars which were survived by the people, but today the populace goes about business and pleasure as usual while "doom" laps at the door.

"London Rain" is one of MacNeice's metaphysical poems, perhaps suggested by the famous "wager scene" of Pascal's *Pensées*. The warning beacons on the English Channel become God and No-God playing at pitch and toss. And unlike Pascal, it makes no difference which one wins. If God wins, He will simply pardon the sinner; if No-God wins "nothing will matter at all." MacNeice wrote "Primrose Hill" in June 1939. Previously, in *Zoo*, he had mentioned the view of the zoological gardens to be obtained from his bachelor apartment. Now the trees have been cut away from the crest of that hill for an antiaircraft emplacement. At times it looks favorably like a life raft tossing in green, leafy seas. At other times he knows the raft will ride in a stormier swell, the sirens will howl, the searchlights will finger the dark, and the "impartial bombs" will fall.

This quiet, pleasant collection ranges in style from the jog-trot rhythms of "Dublin" to the lyricism of "Cushendun." The artist has clearly moved ahead technically; he makes many successful experiments in style, metric, and rhyme pattern. But there is a certain embarrassment at the point of maturation, for too many of the poems are juvenile in topic, mood, and intention. The major tension in the collection lies between the settled, safe past and the threats of war. But it is a dialectic which never proceeds beyond the tension of thesis-antithesis to synthesis. The thought is still arrested at the shock level of *Autumn Journal*. The poems say three things exceedingly well, but the total effect is lost by the complete lack of formulation of the necessary fourth. MacNeice is charming and even poignant at "When I was young"; his nostalgia is most persuasive in "This is the old England I loved"; the shock is much more muted than in the previous diary-journal of "These are the pieces of the past after the bombs burst." But instead of a true climax, with the restoration of order, this is simple catastrophe which leaves the pieces and the audience scattered everywhere. The pieces might be picked up and restored to the old, settled pattern—and this is manifestly impossible. Or they may be put together by a new logic to make a new and better pattern. But the poet doubts that they can be put together in a new pattern, and even more he doubts that such a new pattern would be better than the old one which was bombed. Thus the pieces lie scattered on the floor and the absence of a structure of logic gives the delightfully and eminently readable verse a note of irrelevance and frivolity. It is a mistake to let surface rhythms blind us to the shadow of defeatism in, appropriately, *The Last Ditch*. It is a good thing for a competent artist to re-oil his tools, but where does one go from "the last ditch?"

On August 23, 1939, German Foreign Minister Joachim von Ribbentrop and Vyacheslav M. Molotov, a new Commissioner for Russian Foreign Affairs, signed in Moscow a ten-year Russo-German Nonaggression Pact. The extremes met, the opposites embraced, and the polarity that had produced the supreme tension of the decade sagged into nothing. An epoch which had refused to accept the squalid and expedient present, which had flirted idealistically and passionately with the Millennium, was slain by this act of supreme political cynicism.

4

Wystan Hugh Auden: The Tyranny of Mind

Because of the strength of his personality, the individuality of his poetic gift, and his sheer intellectuality, Auden not only tended to dominate his friends, but also to fascinate them personally and to influence strongly their ideas, if not their styles. C. Day-Lewis wrote about Auden and Stephen Spender in *A Hope for Poetry* (1934). A year later, Stephen Spender discussed his friends in *The Destructive Element* (1935), and again in his autobiography, *World Within World* (1951), as well as in his study of critical theory, *The Creative Element* (1953). Christopher Isherwood, who collaborated with Auden on several plays, is particularly helpful in his recollections of early material about Auden in *Lions and Shadows* (1938). Louis MacNeice, a poet who shared the general enthusiasm for things political, and who collaborated with Auden on two books, said some illuminating things about the group as well as indicating his own areas of agreement and disagreement, in *Modern Poetry* (1938) and in the fragmentary autobiography, *The Strings Are False*, written before 1941 but only published posthumously in 1966. Although he does not discuss the group as such, John Lehmann, in *The Whispering Gallery* (1955), has some revealing things to say about their individual careers from the point of view of a friend, a fellow writer, and a publisher of some of their early work.

Therefore, with all this wealth of commentary by sensitive fellow craftsmen who knew him best, perhaps it is not only appropriate but almost unavoidable that this study should deal with Auden in the terms of a development charted by one of those friends, Stephen Spender, in *World Within World*. Spender points out that at an early age, Auden had an extensive knowledge of the theories of modern psychology, which he used as a means not only of understanding himself, but also of dominating his friends. "He knew what he wanted and he seemed to understand himself, which made him stand out amongst his intelligent but dazed and un-self-knowing friends." [1]

Spender admits that his memory may exaggerate Auden's youthful self-awareness and self-confidence, but he feels sure that he does not exaggerate the impression he made on others. The impression might have been a psychic fraud, but it certainly created a social weakness as surely as it supplied personal strength. "For to know oneself and others too well is a form of realism which risks defeating its own ends. . . . Auden, despite his perceptiveness, lacked something in human relationships. He forced issues too much, made everyone too conscious of himself and therefore was in the position of an observer who is a disturbing force in the behaviour he observes." [2]

Spender felt that Auden sometimes gave the impression of playing an intellectual game with himself and with others, and when the others became aware of the manipulation, the result was social isolation. "His early poetry also gives the impression of an intellectual game—a game to which the name Clinical Detachment might be given. It is a game of impartial objectivity about catastrophes, wars, revolutions, violence, hatreds, loves, and all the forces which move through human lives." But this attitude of the young poet with a bird's-eye view on human calamity in a world of wars and dismantled works runs the risk of becoming facilely inhuman. Auden himself was too human, moreover, for it to be an attitude which he could for long maintain in the face of experiences that wrung his heart. After all, the young poet does become involved, he cannot regard justice and injustice, love and hatred, life and death, with exactly the same impartiality, tracing them with icy precision, like the features of a frozen landscape. "But although Auden ceased to be detached, joined movements, wrote love poetry, accepted the Anglican creed, I am not sure whether he completely broke away from the isolation in human relationships which was simply the result of his overwhelming cleverness as a very young man." [3]

His later work is distinguished from his earlier, says Spender, by the attempt to find answers to what, in the earlier, he is content to state as tremendous questions. "In an early, exceptionally autobiographical poem, he describes himself walking with a friend who speaks of injustice; of someone being murdered, of someone else being 'thrown downstairs,' and so on; and Auden describes himself listening to this, preserving his attitude of detachment in the face of the account of human injustice." It is enough to describe behavior; the clinical observer need not protest, affirm, hold opinions, or try to find an answer. But perhaps this attitude existed only because the young poet was not near enough to the problems stated. [4]

In the next phase that Spender delineates, an answer is rather promiscuously provided—the answer of love. However, this is a love which is supposed to save both the individual who is aware of his own subconscious depths, and the society which has repented of its evil exploitation. It is " 'the sovereign touch' " which can cure even an " 'intolerable neural itch.' " It can connect " 'new styles in architecture' " with a personal and social " 'change of heart' " (Auden, "Petition," poem 30, *Poems*). A bust of Apollo, with the accumulated beauty of the centuries seemed to say to Rilke (*Sonnets to Orpheus*) "You must change your life." To the foul Medusa head of industrial England in the thirties, the Pylon poets made the same demand. They were ready to change their own lives, but they wanted their world to change with them.

But Spender rejects Auden's solution as "too analytic, too adaptable and adjustable to every occasion, too sterilized, too much the love in a psychoanalyst's room. So with the other answers: from psychology to Communism to Christianity; they remain a little arbitrary: and perhaps the root of this arbitrariness is the poet's own isolation." Although

Spender feels that Auden's answers, which have ranged from psychoanalysis, through political revolution and universal love to Christian dogma, have never quite lost their arbitrary, experimental quality, as though they were repeated attempts to understand the nature of a problem, and to solve it by the rearrangement of its elements according to certain hypotheses, Spender freely acknowledges that "nevertheless the problem itself is ever more profoundly understood and brilliantly illustrated. . . . He has an intellectual understanding of situations which he states with his heart as well as his intellect, and if the solution which he offers to the problem seems intellectualized the problem itself is completely realized." [5]

One clear result of the interrelationship of the group is the effect Auden unquestionably had on the diction and imagery of their poetry. It can only be called a "masculinizing" effect, as, to the Romantic-Georgian nature worship of Day-Lewis, the classical decorum of MacNeice, the something effete and decadent in Spender, is added the virile bounce and zest, what MacNeice called the "peasant" quality of Auden. His use of the imagery of the industrial revolution, the fondness for music-hall tunes and rhythms, his tendency toward parody and buffoonery—all had their imitations and echoes in the more traditional, less contemporary, and certainly less intellectual poetry of his friends.

There are at least two areas in which one would like to put limits on Spender's splendidly personal reaction. First, to describe his friend's poetic development as psychology, politics, and Christianity is so simplistic as to fall into the very trap into which he feels Auden fell—arbitrariness. Second, when he speaks of Auden as an intellectual poet who nevertheless "states with his heart as well as his intellect," [6] he brilliantly fulfills T. S. Eliot's description of the feeling brain and the thinking heart of the metaphysical poets—the famous "unified sensibility" theory. But actually a more exact statement of the case would be that Auden feels emotion in the apprehension of the problem and expresses that emotion through image and symbol, but the dissatisfaction that arises from his attempts at solution is rooted in the deficiency that they are usually stated only in terms of intellect. Poem 16 of *Poems* (1930) relates to the problem Spender raised about the preponderance of mind in Auden's poetry. This poem states the poet's analysis of his own tendency: "Living" is always "thinking" to him, although his thoughts may be changed by life and his life changed by thoughts; whereas "feeling" tends to emerge as "seeing." Thought and emotion are not then, for Auden, the unified consciousness of the metaphysicals, but an interior dividedness whereby the critique of life tends to be intellectual while the exterior statement of feeling emerges only in visual terms.

Stephen Spender, in *The Destructive Element*, traced the movement of modern writers from the expression of no belief and pure lyricism, past the outmoded expression of individual belief, to the *summum bonum* of critical interpretation of the existing conditions of man's life and the proposal of political solutions as guides to future specific action and partisanship. Although, at least for a time, Day-Lewis and Spender found both critical interpretation and political solution in communism, Auden seemed simply to reflect an empirical philosophy which could easily be squared with the social materialism of Marx, although he himself appears to have had little interest at any time in practical politics or the joining of parties. Thus, although Spender's division of Auden's work in the 1930s is illuminating even if overly categorical, his judgment of goals is not exactly the judgment of his friend. Perhaps Auden's tongue-in-cheek description of himself in "Letter to Lord Byron" (*Letters from Iceland*) puts it as succinctly and unsparingly as possible: "A selfish pink old Liberal to the last."

Poems (1930) and *The Orators* (1932) quite clearly fall into the category of the diagnosis of a sick and moribund culture. Auden's special theory of illness, as Spender points out in *The Destructive Element*, was based on the psychosomatic theories of Homer Lane, to whom all illness is a manifestation of the death wish. *Poems* was dedicated to Christopher Isherwood with the ambiguous sentiment in rhyming quatrain that we should learn to honor vertical men, although in actual fact we value only horizontal ones. If verticality is taken in the context of illness, then we should honor health and dishonor sickness, although in actual fact, our culture, which is sick itself, does just the opposite. If verticality is considered in the context of political analysis, then we should honor the radical critic rather than the supine conformist, although, again, the tendency of the world is precisely the opposite.

The first entry in *Poems* is a charade "Paid On Both Sides," dedicated to C. Day-Lewis. In slightly archaic language and a sparse diction like the "telegraphese" of Browning, the drama tells of a feud between the Nowers and the Shaws, which John Nower attempts to heal by marrying Anne Shaw. However this Romeo-Juliet solution of the difficulties of two warring houses—a Shaw has just been killed by a Nower—is frustrated by Seth Shaw, who, at his mother's instigation—often in the poems of the Oxford poets, the mother represents unthinking traditionalism as well as complete possessiveness—murders John, leaving his own sister a pregnant widow. It had been John Nower, however, who sent George and Sturton to get Shaw and to kill him from ambush at the ford.

In "Paid On Both Sides" the conflict is not the psychological conflict of the divided mind, but the cultural topography of an endless, mindless, meaningless feud between two families, neither one a whit better than the other, a blind struggle in the dark from which only Dick escapes by emigration. At first John, George, and Sturton are forced into death-dealing action by the murky information of a traitor. Then, having thus paid their due to the past and admitted the inevitability of continual conflict, John, through love, attempts to solve the conflict by marriage and new birth—a child who will be both Nower and Shaw. But this hope is frustrated by the mother figure (as in *The Ascent of F6* and Day-Lewis's *Transitional Poem*) whose central loyalty is to the past, to the loss of her own son, and who thus primordially cries out that blood demands blood. So at the end nothing is better. The new life will

presumably be tainted by family memories of past treacheries. The only way to cut oneself free from the past is by
migration, by moving into another context or culture. Memory brings death; only by the loss of memory can men be
reborn.

The Man-Woman in the charade is a kind of biological
syndrome which gives force to evolutionary process. If
finally, in disgust, it passes on to other forms of life, mankind will be doomed. Thus man controls his own fate, for
he premises the acceptance or rejection of the Man-Woman.
Man-Woman claims that it has tried to make this presently
moribund society flourish, but society either rejected its aid
or twisted its offers into promiscuity, masturbation, and the
Oedipus complex. But it may already be too late, as this
charade suggests and as poem 3 states: the Man-Woman
will pass on the other side and choose some other favorite.

In the delightful banter between the doctor and his
apprentice, we discover that this is a culture which has
produced no Sigmund Freud or Homer Lane; all this doctor
can cure is tennis elbow, Derbyshire neck, Housemaid's
knee—in other words, the trivia of a fussy, crotchety society. When he examines the dead body of the spy, he notes
that cerebrally the spy was suffering from a dominant intellect which made satisfying emotional life impossible. Perhaps the poet jocularly confesses his own limitation. Although John's attempt toward solution by the power of love
was a step in the right direction, it had about it the defeat
of an incomplete decision. For John has not understood
that even love cannot flourish within a sick society, and the
lover certainly does not have the power to redeem. Thus in
two possible directions the charade is tragic: if it is an
allegory of a man's inner conflict played out with all the
stage props of natural scenery and two families, then the
moral is simply that banishment of the unhealthy forces in
his own psyche is inadequate. If instead, it is to be taken as
the saga of a social feud, then the tragic element comes
from the inadequacy of individual rebirth within a moribund social structure. John could not realize that his very
health would make him seem perverse and an enemy to the

ill. They would have to kill him in order to preserve the lie of their own normality.

In the poetry of this Freud-conscious group, the mother-son relationship often serves as a symbol of the power of the past, the claim of nature that excludes the mind, the obsessive need of one person to survive by owning other persons, and a final betrayal of all pioneer instincts in the radical individual. In Auden and Isherwood's *The Ascent of F6*, the mountain climber's mother betrays him at first by a lie and finally destroys him by the truth. In Spender's *Return to Vienna*, the martyred hero is betrayed by the kisses of his sweetheart and his mother. In Day-Lewis's *Transitional Poem*, the Defendant is a mother who seems to assert the claims of the natural life, but is actually seeking a transfusion of youthful blood to aid her own longevity. In Day-Lewis's *A Time to Dance*, one of the protagonist's enemies is his wife, another his mother.

As in *The Magnetic Mountain*, Day-Lewis took a private engine back along the loop to examine the land from which they have come, so in poem 22 Auden invites us to survey the land we once were proud of and now will find only a museum of abandoned factories. It is quite true that after World War I until the formation of the National Government in 1931, more parliamentary debate was concerned with unemployment than any other topic. In the average interwar year, 14.4 percent of the working population were unemployed. A survey by Mark Abrams indicated that in the first years of the 1930s one out of five workers was unemployed, and that this percentage increased alarmingly after the middle of the decade. Twenty years later Stephen Spender named unemployment as the major issue which drew intellectuals of the period into communism. So in Auden's *Poems* the uncompleted tramline runs out in the woods (11), industry is comatose, the gates of the factories are shut tight (21), even the power stations stand deserted (22). Spender spoke of men with dull cigarettes, standing idle beside the roads. And Day-Lewis, in "A Carol," wrote satirically about the baby of the poor whose cradle is in the pawnshop, whose mother is in tears, and whose father is on the dole.

In the twenty-second poem, Auden also refers to money invested abroad while the companies in which Britons invested were surreptitiously underselling their own investors. The Edwardian period had great affluence, but British wealth was largely invested abroad while home labor conditions remained unimproved and the tools of production became obsolete. So unless labor emigrated along with the capital, the affluence of the period went unshared by the workers. Here is the economic fact that lies behind the emigration of Dick in "Paid On All Sides." When the workers in poem 22 ask what they can do to remedy the situation, all they can see are frivolous alternatives: athletics on the village green after working hours, long hours spent in public houses, hunting in fields and forests. They stand dazed with a sense that the poets of the period share, that the decisions and actions that were simple and clear to their ancestors are vague and confused to them (cf. Spender's poem "Exiles").

Poem 21 describes the descendants of aristocratic families and of economic tycoons as facades, going through the proper forms of behavior, but centrally weak and confused. In poem 18, these descendants are gently described as comely and pleasant. Yet everything that was once part of the life of a united family making real history has now become vain repetition of worn-out forms. By analogy to evolution, poem 3 suggests that the basic problem is a refusal to change. These are the true decadents, Auden seems to be saying, these stern pillars of the status quo who hold a single position forever, who can be completely wrong with such dignified conviction. Poem 28 repeats the theme of evolutionary types which refused to adapt to changing conditions of life and were thus eliminated, and uses them as the analogues of a ruling class that refuses to develop new characteristics. Here the genetic pattern, repeated until it becomes recessive, is seen as public evidence of a class death wish. Poem 29 transforms genes and chromosomes into the traditional religious figure of a "supreme antagonist" (Louis MacNeice's God and No-God in "London Rain") who has the task of killing off unhealthy societies. So modern men might look at their clogged harbors and run-down factories and recognize the evidence that they are now producing their own graves. Although this is true of the culture as a whole, once again there are such exceptions as migratory Dick of "Paid On Both Sides," for the Antagonist may choose to go to a portside bar and beckon his chosen one to walk out across the sunlit water. Although this poem avoids the determinism of genetics, it falls into the older determinism of predestination by mentioning the favorites of the Adversary, fore-chosen and foreordained.

Poems 28 and 29 return to the pattern of men who cause their own downfall by their stubborn, self-righteous refusal to change to fit new times. The death wish appears in a culture which is already moribund; when an old society has become completely rigid, it becomes necessary to destroy the old in order to make way for the new. Replogle has pointed out that Auden had picked up through his omnivorous reading the theory of a life-force or power called "It" which lives through the individual lives or organisms.[7] Auden referred jocularly to Professor Georg Groddeck's theory in his "Letter to Byron," by wondering what on earth the "It" was thinking when it gave him such flat feet and such a "big behind." Now, more seriously, it may be considered the secular twin of the Supreme Antagonist who will kill off the present failed generation by both infection and neurosis.

This idea of historical cleansing by means of infection and neurosis can be traced to Auden's admiration for the psychological theories of Homer Lane. Christopher Isherwood illuminates the discussion by his explanation of Lane's theory of automatic prophylaxis: "If the conscious mind were really the controlling factor, the world would become bedlam in a few generations, and the race would automatically die out. . . . Diseases are therefore only warning symptoms of a sickness of the soul. . . . the disease of the soul is the belief in moral control: the Tree of the Knowledge of Good and Evil, as against the Tree of Life."[8] Since Isherwood derived his understanding of Lane at second hand, and since he greatly admired D. H. Lawrence, one is prepared for the slightly Lawrentian flavor even in the explanation of another figure. But this passage not only describes the thought of Homer Lane, it is also a close parallel to Marxist social theory, illustrating how easily Auden could slip into the framework of Marxist dialectic without serious dislocation or soul-searching agony. Communism assumes that all social forms change inevitably. These changes include a recognition that the inner contradictions of a culture grow sharper with time, the class struggle arises, and one social form changes into another, not by easy transition, for it is contradictoriness with which we are dealing, but by catastrophic revolution.

Poem 16 is a dramatic rehearsal of all the traumas the individual suffers as he passes from birth to maturity. The baby, warm and protected in the intimate relationship of the womb, is ejected into the world, afraid and alone. Inner conflicts weaken him; unfair conditions keep him from self-realization. He attempts to fool himself by denying that the conflict exists. But the unforgiving hostility he has suppressed now takes its revenge, so that instead of learning to love others, he develops both hatred of others and love of death. The body knows sex, but not love. Poem 9 is a dramatic monologue by a neurotic adult who has experienced this kind of societal repression. He finds the seat of the will at the base of his spine. The mind desires, but the nerves which should carry the message have been severed by the world, therefore the body is unable to follow its own normal instinctual impulses. The resultant condition is a double invalidism—inability to comprehend or to act. The original beginnings of his neurosis were rooted in a too-close relationship with his mother. Poem 4 paints a portrait of an extremely competent and sophisticated member of the upper class; but this exterior is based on an interior balancing act which threatens to collapse at any moment. In the last stages of a doomed culture, although society displays no new piety, individuals such as this decadent aristocrat may seek religion as an escape. Poem 3 simply suggests that in these cases the religious escape is undifferentiated from the death wish.

In poem 24 tourists seek heroes who will deliver them

from their boring and unfulfilled lives (cf. Mr. and Mrs. A in *The Ascent of F6*). But just like those who retreat to the chapels and hills to pray, the tourists are really indulging in fantasies which are further evidence of their neurotic state. Auden tells them unequivocally that all the true leaders have left the countryside to gather at "Cape Wrath"—there to prepare for the coming world cataclysm.

With the same general idea, poem 2 portrays a man who has the courage to leave although he carries his old dreams and memories with him. In the final stanza of the poem, there is a petition for the ultimate success of this traveler. May he be saved from capture, from sudden death; may he be able to complete the full process of rebirth in the new land. But will this individual triumph have the power to transform an old culture? Poem 1 asks whether it is possible to make a thoroughgoing critique of a culture, to find it lacking both in actual health and the very possibility of health, without being forced into some violent ending.

Although the dramatic dialogue form of many of Auden's poems makes it dangerous to identify the poet with a speaker, and although the poem thoroughly explores both sides of the issue—to stay or to leave—still it points out the logical contradiction involved in condemning a social order and yet remaining a part of it. He recognizes the personal nausea involved in going off to war; it is hard to be patriotic when you are convinced that wars are fought for nothing. He recognizes and admits the attractiveness of sexual activity as a substitute for social criticism.

As solution for all this malaise, the poet seems to have to offer only the emigration theme, the theme of heroic isolation, and the very same theme of love which he had already clearly shown to be ineffective in "Paid On All Sides." Both poems 13 and 14 return to this discredited theme of love. Poem 27 admits that it is easy to ask hard questions, but answers are both hard to find and hard to remember. Hard to find in the sense of real and effective solutions; hard to remember in the sense that men seem unable to profit by their evolutionary past, and thus sink back into the ways from which they came. If men could only remember the instinctual behavior which is natural to them, they might then finally recover the power to love. In poem 26 the vision has somehow faded and everything seems to have become disappointing and unsatisfactory. Yet even in this poem, there are celebrated a few fleeting moments of love. Although J. S. Southworth pointed out the homosexual element in much of the early poetry of Auden, actually the sexual object makes little difference to Auden's concept of love as passion or quiet joy briefly snatched from the phenomena of a hostile world which, like a procession, constantly moves by. Brief and promiscuous though these contacts may be, they are still worthy to be valued for themselves.

The theme of violent ending of the old is certainly present in these poems. Poem 22 asks if things have already gone too far for any revolution to cleanse? Doom is so close that the public-school, cocktail-drinking, tennis-playing class must shut their mouths and quit charming everybody with their haberdashery, or the working class will blow everything sky high. Here the revolution is clearly class war, the workers against the upper classes, with the intellectuals destroyed in between. Poem 16 states flatly that the world needs the death of all "the old gang."

The Orators: An English Study (1932) should be linked with *Poems* in consideration of its tendency to work out many of the themes first found there. Dedicated to Stephen Spender, it opens with a prologue which expresses much the same problem Day-Lewis had expressed: this is the reward of the prophetic poet who dares to criticize existing conditions, to prophesy immediate destruction, and to project future social beatitude—his mother will call him a deceiver and the crowds will consider him a coward. In a foreword to later editions, no doubt with the famous Auden tongue somewhere in the ubiquitous Auden cheek, he wrote: "As a rule, when I re-read something I wrote when I was younger, I can think myself back into the frame of mind in which I wrote it. *The Orators*, though, defeats me. My name on the title-page seems a pseudonym for someone else, someone talented but near the border of sanity, who might well, in a year or two, become a Nazi."

It would be hard to find a better example of the unmitigated nonsense authors have often written about their own work. But the paragraph which follows returns to a more factual statement of the literary influences which were brought to play on *The Orators*: Eliot pointed out to Auden the debt of "Argument and Statement" to the *Anabase* of St. John Perse. "Journal of an Airman" was inspired by the new translation of Baudelaire's *Journals Intimes* by Christopher Isherwood, Auden informs us, plus "a very dotty semi-autobiographical book by General Ludendorff, the title of which I have forgotten. And over the whole work looms the shadow of that dangerous figure, D. H. Lawrence the Idealogue, author of *Phantasia of the Unconscious* and those sinister novels *Kangaroo* and *The Plumed Serpent*."

In the same foreword, Auden identifies the central theme of *The Orators* as hero worship (cf. Day-Lewis's theme of hero worship) and immediately apologizes for the political implications of fascism. "My guess today is that my unconscious motive in writing it was therapeutic, to exorcise certain tendencies in myself by allowing them to run riot in phantasy."

Book 1 is entitled "The Initiates" and has to do with an education which does not fit youth for the realities of the present world, a theme as old-fashioned as Meredith's *Ordeal of Richard Feverel* and as modern as Joyce's *Portrait of the Artist as a Young Man*. "Address for a Prize-Day" is a marvel of heavy-handed satire. The poet starts by asking questions: What were the dead like, what sort of people are we today, why are we here, what are we going to do? Then comes the major question of the volume and perhaps the major issue of Auden's poetry of the decade, "What do you think about this England, this country of ours where nobody is well?" [9] One is immediately reminded of the famous dialogue in which Aldous Huxley published a pamphlet in 1936 entitled *What Are You Going to Do About It? The Case for Constructive Peace*, and C. Day-Lewis replied *We're Not Going To Do Nothing* in November of the same year.

Taking his levels of sin from Dante's *Inferno*, Auden discusses first those who have been guilty of excessive love of themselves, the children who play in their own corner, shy, lonely, bird-watchers, long before the mirror, indefatigable readers, prone to illnesses which close vision and hearing. At school they stay far from the study fire, are no earthly use in games, and thereby unpopular. The second group are excessive lovers of their neighbors—they care far too much. Actually the need is for calm friendship and quiet love. Next are the defective lovers who are characterized by inertia; they are collectors of trivia and their lives are full of unacted desires. Last are the perverted lovers; haters of life, they are terrified to die. Who could have made them this way? Not parents or schoolmasters, but the well adapted, the popular, the boys who have ambition but are never stirred by dreams. What should be done with the popular who have twisted the lives of the unpopular? Throw them in the Black Hole under the floor of the dining hall of the school where new boys are always initiated. If left there, they will produce no popular children to warp less attractive peers. The section ends with rousing but frightening orders: "Well, look to it. Quick, guard that door. Stop that man. Good. Now boys hustle them, ready, steady—go."

"Argument" is the fantasy of boys forming secret clubs, playing robbers and mock revolutionaries. There is a mythic hero, "Him," to whom all seven boys are bound in absolute obedience. Each of the seven has a special talent which can be useful for revolutionary espionage. In their fantasy, the boys become invisible to their parents, they cross frontiers, they choose up guides for passing through gorges. The boys talk about generals in paneled English rooms, they find suspicious traces of grit on goggles which were presents from their aunts. They plan special questions with clever verbal traps for interrogating the villagers. They execute a spy in back of the cow barn. They write their fantastic reports to Him in the evenings; to Him they have absolute devotion. They have no time for girls because their time is spent in serious missions.

Section 2 is a litany of petition naming each of the seven boys and asking deliverance from his particular weakness. Then follows such nursery-rhyme names for each, as Cat with the Fiddle, Bull at the Gate, and the Seven against Thebes. However at the point when the names end, there is a shift from the personal weaknesses of the seven boys to the weaknesses of their class and their culture which also require elimination.

Section 3 increases in seriousness as one of the seven is found, face downward on a wet road, in the early morning. The six suspect one of their number of having delivered him over to the hatred of the "villas." But the basic problem develops within the seven themselves, as they forget their absolute vows of fealty to their Leader and begin to fall in love with death.

"Argument" seems the selection most open to the accusation of Fascist tendencies of which the author warned in his foreword: "We all know what . . . [hero worship] can lead to," and in ascribing its authorship to "someone . . . who might well, . . . become a Nazi." In the authority that he exercises over his early friends (Isherwood, *Lions and Shadows*; Spender, *World Within World*; John Lehmann, *The Whispering Gallery*), it is possible that Auden recognized in himself a kind of fuehrer complex and that this poem was his way of exposing it in order to rid himself of it, or as he puts it in the foreword: "to exorcise certain tendencies in myself by allowing them to run riot in phantasy."

"Statement" is quite different in tone, but with some similarity in theme. The Heraclitean idea "Life is many" is repeated in section 1 as the introductory section claims that every life has a place and an award. There follows a catalogue of the special qualities, aptitudes, and abilities that individuals possess. The second section proceeds to list the penalties endemic within each ability. But in addition to listing tragic endings, it also mentions those who have been remarkably saved from such erosion of character. The end of the poetic prose shows the specific weakness of various species along the evolutionary line, and closes with an analysis of man in terms of vocation: man, woman, child, friend, boys and girls, the old, the leader, the followers, the muscular, etc. The last two lines claim that light has the power to make darkness contract, perhaps indebted to the Greek idea that dark and light are palpable substances, so that if light is to enter, dark must contract (cf. "The light shines in the darkness, and the darkness has not overcome it." Gospel According to John 1:5 [R.S.V.]). To the poet the contraction of darkness was the necessary prelude both to artistic creativity and social inventiveness. For one who was constantly diagnosing a sick society, it is surprising that Auden could strike so jocular a mood in "Letter to a Wound" which is exactly what the title suggests, a love letter from a convalescent to the incision left after an operation.

Book 2 "Journal of an Airman" is the most considerable part of *The Orators*. With less precious and private "coterie talk" than book 1, the title is a reminder of the group's interest in fliers and planes (Day-Lewis's kestrel and Stephen Spender's airplanes), the perfect union of modern mechanics and intellectual aspiration. The introductory comment is rather close to the Marxist explanation of the function of war in a multi-classed capitalistic society. If left to itself, Auden says, an organism will organize itself naturally. But the enemy (the established powers) introduce "inert velocities" which may be defined as laws and habits which interfere with natural organization. These produce a spiritual friction which ignites international and civil war. There follow several geometric theorems with diagrams concerning the relationships possible to likes and dislikes.

The poem in *Note* 2 repeats a theme common to *Poems*, that the first generation of British leadership was proud, paid its debts, but the second generation is in every way unworthy of its ancestors. A genetic diagram in the preceding *Note* leads Auden to deduce that the true ancestor may be an uncle or a great-grandfather, followed by the notation that his mother had always disliked his uncle.

The enemy of free men, he claims, is full of half-truths; compare the accuracy of his description of symptoms with the stupidity of his prescriptions. A dog is sick, hind legs paralyzed, we must help him walk again, so a tablespoonful of arsenic is administered three times daily. But the dog has been suffering all along from arsenic poisoning. Thus in his sick culture, adept at analysis, but inept at synthesis, the cure turns out to be exactly the same as the disease. The progress of the disease is so rapid that it may already be too late, since gangrene has set in. Auden's Uncle Sam appears again in this section full of the intimate jokes of a little ingroup who knew each other at Marlborough School and Oxford and have their own little nicknames and private laughs. After a rather tepid Airmen's Alphabet, the enemy is described as immaculately dressed, good conversationalists who generally make the appeal to home and duty. There follows a rather random series of traits of the enemy arranged in groups of three. After the "coterie talk" common to Auden and MacNeice, the most irritating characteristic of the volume is a series of unrelated observations taken from Auden's daybook and stated in an aphoristic manner, such as "Trains keep stopping regular as dogs by certain posts."

Then a major section on his uncle is introduced. When Auden was sixteen and a half, his uncle invited him to dine at his flat and gave him champagne for dinner. When he left that night, the poet knew who and what he was because he had discovered his "real ancestor." The newspaper notice that Derek crashed his plane and was killed reminds the reader of the frequent place of sudden and violent death in the writings of Auden. During the elegy for Derek, the poet calls for a significant change of heart, and points out that the strength of the enemy is that most people believe there is no real danger. Then the poet lists the definitions by negatives that the enemy always purveys and that mar the lives of youth: *unless* you do well you shall *not* be loved; *afraid* of death (instead of wanting to live), pleasure as the *decrease* of pain. The enemy likes to ask why anyone would want to think and talk about a coming war—isn't that being militaristic?

From this point on, one gathers that things have come to the point of open hostility between the airmen and the enemy. A ridiculous accusation of a prominent citizen in the *Courier* becomes meaningful when the reader recognizes that the article describes the crimes of the whole upper-middle class: arson, coining, dozing in public office, espionage, heresy, false news statements, jingoism, mental cruelty, nepotism, onanism, quixotry, sabotage, tea-drinking, unnatural offenses against children, etc. On the twenty-fifth day the airman asks what he has written in his diary and he replies: "Thoughts suitable to a sanatorium," another reference to the warning of the foreword, "near the border of sanity."

Book 3 of *The Orators* contains six odes. In the first, the poet hears a voice inviting Auden, Spender, and Isherwood to tally up the total of their losses in the past year. Spender cries " 'Destroy this temple' " and Isherwood shivers to think that " 'man is a spirit.' " In the great world the poet sees no one with power, but he sees the beggar nations of earth in terms of coming and sure power. Ode 2 praises Gabriel Carrit, Captain of Sedbergh School, for the Spring victory over Sandroyd in 1927. Excited and pleasant, it has only one social comment, that heroes though they be in their school days, later on, inexplicably but irretrievably, they will be "sold." Above the joy of a holiday with friends, ode 3, to Edward Upward, schoolmaster and writer, contains ominous hints, sad postures, slight despairs, gin in a drawer, and the shadow of death. Ode 4 is a longer work dedicated to John Warner, son of Rex and Frances Warner. John Bull is worried about his island, and well he might be, for a walk through her cities reveals the plight of the "proletariat": ugly, dirty, stewing around in idleness, slacking on the job, voyeurs of other people making love in the park or on the screen, empty-minded, uninteresting, and hopeless. But an examination of the upper class proves only that they too "won't pass." Who can save England? MacDonald, Hoover, Baldwin, and Briand all claim they are giants but are pygmies in fact. Mussolini, Pilsudski, and Hitler are noisy and boring. Youth will save England, say the bishops, the teachers, and the Sunday *Express*. But the young people they depend upon are mostly "dummies" who want their mothers and are afraid of their fathers. Who will save England? Children like John, son of Warner. Now is the season, in the face of falling wages and the falling value of the British pound, for a "change of heart" which will unite the nation, poor and rich, employed and idle, town and country.

Ode 5 is addressed to Auden's former pupils who are now in army camps. He speaks angrily of the deceits that put them there and reveals that the enemy against whom they fight is really the downtrodden poor of their own land. They are trained by the Seven Deadly Sins and they must not imagine that simple interpersonal love will stop the carnage. They are doomed to attack—but never the right foe. Ode 6 is a shorter poem asking God occasionally to illuminate the minds of men and not always be content just to kill them. In the epilogue, the reader speaks words of fear, terror, and warning to the writer, whose bravery is that he pays them no heed.

Auden dedicated *The Dance of Death* (1933) to Robert Medley and Rupert Doone. From the opening speech of the announcer to the last lines of Karl Marx, the drama is explicitly political. The central theme is the "decline of a class." Although the members of that class dream about a new and richer life, they secretly desire the old familiar world. Instead of being turned toward the future, they are dominated by an unadmitted death wish. Thus the chief actor-dancer of the medley is identified as "death."

The chorus begins with a massive striptease, dropping silk dressing gowns, revealing two-piece bathing suits and a medicine ball. Clearly Dr. Auden's first prescription for the world's malaise is sunshine. The dancer solos as Sun God, creator and destroyer, but the chorus of bathers returns from their plunge in the sea, chilled, clammy, and feeling old. They belatedly seek the warmth of their street clothes, but the dancer has stolen them. In response to their shivered complaints, the Yiddish theater manager offers them costumes from an old musical comedy as substitutes. Ominously the date of the revue was 1916 and all the costumes are miscellaneous uniforms. Surprisingly the song they are expected to sight-read is " 'Soldiers of the King of Kings,' " more expectedly the title of the revue is *The Lady of the Guard*. The audience leaps up to protest that the

Kellogg pact has outlawed war; they desire to spend their money for scholarships, not battleships. A character named Alpha shifts the focus by claiming that all old wars were attacks on the working class. There is a jolly little chorus about the last war being a "bosses' war" and how common men must rise up and build a "workers' state" in which the factories will be seized and operated by the workers themselves. But as Plato in *The Republic* and Wordsworth in *Cintra* had claimed, the revolution of the people only leads to the rule of the demogogue—the people's friend. The announcer, ostensibly agreeing that a revolution may now be necessary, insinuates that it cannot be a revolution on the Russian pattern, but on English lines, not to create one class but no class, "Englishmen for Englishmen." So the revolution shifts to recrudescent nationalism, with overtones of fascism, particularly when the announcer denounces the theater manager as a "dirty Jew," and helps the crowd beat him up.

In the next episode, the men decide that they can get along very nicely without women. Meanwhile they return to preadolescence and form a gigantic, glorified boy scout troop. This denial of sexuality edges quickly into a mystical search for the ideal. Now the dancer becomes the intrepid pilot flying to the very heart of reality. But in the midst of the flight, the dancer falls, paralyzed. Thereupon the manager gives up the theater business and opens a cosy little night club just like home called "The Alma Mater." The search for the ideal has fallen into the most banal folksiness. But the dancer has achieved his secret goal and has died happily.

Enter Mr. Karl Marx, hailed by the chorus singing to the melody of Mendelssohn's "Wedding March," asking him to explain all their acts on the basis of economic materialism. Looking at the corpse of the dancer, Marx—whom Philip Henderson claimed to be Groucho, not Karl—proclaims that the instruments of production were too much for the dancer to handle; therefore there was nothing to do but to liquidate him. Marx exits to the band playing the "Dead March" from *Saul*.

The longing of the people for a better life along with

their incipient death wish, their interests in physical culture, the safe past, a workers' revolution, nationalism, fascism, asceticism, and idealism are all clear and dramatically presented. But the closing remarks of Karl Marx are so parodic that they refuse to be taken seriously and so the whole thing ends with the old tongue-in-cheek suspicion that we are being spoofed. A use of buffoonery, set to music-hall tunes, to state serious truths has cleansing value in the face of the customary pomposity, but the joke at the end makes it difficult to discuss the drama in any very serious reference.

John Lehmann, who obtained several of Auden's best lyrics for the early issues of *New Writing*, suggests an interesting but highly controversial analysis of Auden's development: "By the time he started contributing to *New Writing* he had outgrown the arcane doom-laden telegraphese of his first book and *Paid on Both Sides*; had passed very rapidly through the phase of the bullying, Marxist bogey-man exhortations and emerged unscathed into the clear sunlight—so clear that it is only necessary to recite two or three of them to silence anyone who complains that modern poetry is too obscure and esoteric to bother about, —the midsummer's day of his genius. In that full-flowering moment, feeling, thought and technical mastery were, it seems to me, in perfect balance; before his passion for rhetorical personification of abstractions like 'glory,' 'desire,' 'hunger,' 'the will,' began to devour his invention, and the transplantation to America dried up the sensuous sap and made his utterances for a time seem more like the delphic riddling of a disembodied mind." [10]

In collaboration with Christopher Isherwood, W. H. Auden wrote a play, *The Dog Beneath the Skin, or Where Is Francis?* (1935), and dedicated it to Robert Moody. The basic gimmick of the drama is ingeniously removing the village squire's son, letting him reappear in the village wearing a dog's skin, and viewing the insanity of the human world from a stance of canine sanity. Like so many of the poems by the group, it begins with a survey of the state of England—always found to be bad: falling barns, broken fences, great houses only half inhabited, farmers migrating to more hopeful countries, youth gone to city and suburb. The tourists who take their places desire petrol from rustic pumps, live on dividends in ancient cottages with a pet animal or a volume of memoirs, and, of course, never marry and produce heirs. It is too easy to say with the early Auden, Virginia Woolf, and the Bloomsbury group that all that is needed is a change of heart. Auden snorts that to Bloomsbury a change of heart is always solidly based on five hundred pounds income a year and a comfortable room of one's own.

Act 2 takes place in a lunatic asylum, appropriate representative of an insane world. Alan (secondary protagonist) is a prisoner who is forced to watch a parody of fascism with its cult of absolute leadership, its racial prejudice, its emphasis upon the development of the body. In Paradise Park he meets a poet who is too precious and refined to use the common native language. In a sanatorium he meets women whose incipient death wish is revealed by their excited exhibition of their surgical incisions.

In the Ninevah Hotel, Alan falls in love with Miss Vipond, a store dummy, showing the unreality of middle-class culture and its expression of the death wish in narcissistic love (act 3 scene 4). Sir Francis Crewe, after his years as a village dog and traveling about with Alan, finally returns to his village of Pressan Ambo where he is expected to take up again the responsibilities of birth and class that he had thrown aside. But instead, he insults the townspeople with his dog's eye view of the villagers: "obscene, cruel, hypocritical, mean, vulgar." Nevertheless, now that he has returned from wandering with Alan in the great world, he no longer really hates and despises his neighbors. He sees them as companies in a vast army that do not even know that they have been drafted. And he is sure of just one thing—he wants to be fighting on the other side. So starting with a change of landscape and environment, a new Francis demands action which is real and physical. The play ends as Alan and Francis stride off to join the workers' movement with its key words on their lips: Repent—Unite —Act. This abrupt departure takes Alan away from his youthful sweetheart, but the times are too serious for personal romance. The Chorus instructs the audience not to mourn for Alan and Francis who have chosen their lot, but to mourn for themselves who make no choices and are perpetually unable to make up their minds. Finally Francis's criticism of the villagers turns upon himself: wasn't he substituting passive observation for action? Observation is acceptable to Auden as clinical preparation for cure, but not as substitute for deed. The problem of action is central both to Auden and Marx. Man controls his environment and thus his own nature and destiny by empirical criticism and by changing his conduct to fit the diagnosis.

When Auden advocates the change of society by the change of environment (even the total evasion of emigration) he is most at one with Spender and Day-Lewis. But it is notable that at the very same time the former emphasis upon the cathartic necessity of violence is toned down. This leads to the suspicion that the violence which is usually assumed to inhere in any class revolution may really be drawing its power from psychological repression and frustration. If this is so, why not leave the whole matter up to psychiatric therapy? But this solution is rejected because the cure seems to have produced no observable results in the conduct of individual men or the formation of an improved society.

The Ascent of F6: A Tragedy in Two Acts (1936) is perhaps the most considerable play penned by the two collaborators. Dedicated to John Bicknell Auden, it reiterates the by-now-familiar themes of the hero who dares to be different, but is ultimately victimized by his own death wish, the international follies of national leadership, the idealistic quest related to a mountain, the betrayal of men by their own mothers, and man's power to choose among alternatives.

Michael Forsyth Ransom, the mountain-climber, has a twin brother, Sir James Ransom, who is politically as successful as his brother is socially shy and recessive. Michael, who has chosen the pioneering, unpopular path, will be used by his brother and his government for a symbolic victory over a competing nation. He will also be exploited by the press as an anodyne to drug Mr. and Mrs. A so they will forget the boredom of their unfulfilled, unheroic lives. Ian Shawcross, exhuding confidence but feeling miserable uncertainty, claims the penalty of rejection and throws himself off the mountain. David Gunn is the usual silly weak British character who turns out to be marvelously heroic under stress.

Ransom sets the mood of scene 1 by reading, from Dante's *Inferno*, Ulysses' speech about men not being formed to live like brutes, but to follow virtue and knowledge. He considers the seedy adventurers whom Ulysses addressed, a "crook speaking to crooks." But the times are even worse today, so bad that the miscarriage or the corpse can be grateful for their escape. For it is no longer the growth and maturity of the plant that is in question, "the great ordered flower itself" is withering. The situation in fictional divided Sudoland is remarkably like the later dilemma of the United States in Viet Nam, in which America did not dare to withdraw as it wished, because of fear of a Communist take-over.

So far as mother love is concerned, first Mrs. Ransom betrays her son by false assurance that he had always been the strong twin, able to stand alone, therefore not needing her love. This motivates him to engage in a political act about which he has the gravest reservations. The second betrayal comes when, at the very end, she permits him to know the truth that she always preferred her popular son.

In the intensely interesting confrontation between the Abbot and Ransom (act 2, scene 1), the Abbot warns Ransom that no one can kill the demon of the mountain because he is a continuing part of every man's life. He knows Ransom's temptation is to be like James, "great among men." But Michael has always had a charismatic leadership that draws men to enormous devotion because of their desire for self-immolation. If he climbs the mountain he will become a national hero, he will be given power, and inevitably he will be corrupted by it. The Abbot offers an alternative: let him turn from the life of action and glory to the life of contemplation and knowledge in the monastery (cf. the shift from workers' revolution to ascetic mysticism in *Dance of Death*). This is a frontier where the demon, which cannot be slain, can be controlled and limited to the desert wasteland. Actually Ransom does not so much choose as surge on with the momentum of events. Too late comes his repentance for the death of Lamp the botanist, Shawcross the ambitious, Gunn the weak —all sacrifices to his pride. His own death will be used to strengthen nationalism—"once again Englishmen have been weighed in the balance and not found wanting" (act 2, scene 5)—to increase the circulation of the *Evening Moon*, and to give vicarious excitement to the dull lives of suburbanites.

The figure of Michael Ransom is in many ways similar to the Airman in *The Orators*. A member of the upper class, he has broken away, but not far enough to join the lower class, only to slip down one notch into the middle class. His heroic stature is weakened by his jealousy of his brother, his desire to shape himself to fit the mold of another man's life, and his terrible longing for primacy in his mother's affections. Day-Lewis observed that Michael might have been drawn from T. E. Lawrence. He also found himself in total disagreement with Auden if the Abbot was the author's spokesman. He considered the Tibetan cleric's offer of knowledge in contemplation to be so negative that it was only another expression of the death wish. If the Abbot is right, then this is a religious play and the drama of a good man's difficult decisions takes place on the stage of his own individual soul. Michael Ransom represents the Kierkegaardian concept of man as essentially a sinner who can find no way to be pleasing to God. His chief concern is not his nation, his brother, his mother, or his friends. His chief concern is the salvation of his soul and the achievement of a proper relationship with God.

Look, Stranger! published in London, 1936, was dedicated to Auden's wife, Erika Mann. Auden's emphasis upon "external disorder" moves the poems outward from psychological analysis to a recognition of the increasing seriousness of the times. The world is so full of the extravagence, lies, and violence that the poet is left treasuring "narrow strictness" of statement and feeling, a sentiment which is given considerable discussion in poem 30, written to Christopher Isherwood.

The prologue is in the form of a rather traditional invocation to the muse that love might make man's heart beat more simply; that love might display its power in the British islands; that, just as when Newton watched the apple falling toward England's earth and so found a lasting tie between his ideas and his land, so may we find such a tie of love for England. So heartfelt and emotional is Auden's feeling in this volume for the England that, despite all, he loves. The prologue proceeds to ask that some dream which has a possibility of working may silence our talk, pain our kindness, and move out of the future into the actual happenings of today. In poem 2, to Geoffrey Hoyland, the poet confesses that the things they have known and loved together have little power left. Foreseeing a flood pushing its way through men's little contentments, he asks that they may forgive the coming invasion of privacies and cancellation of individualities for the sake of its obvious social values.

Auden returns to an evolutionary theme in poem 3. Our huntsmen ancestors pitied the limitations of animals and saw that something raged inside them from lack of brain. Who would have guessed that the coming men would snarl up the fine liberal tradition in confusion and guilt and would be forced to turn back to poverty, hunger, illegal activities, anonymous selfhood?

In poem 5 the title poem of the volume, Auden again invites the reader to examine his island, but for once the view is remarkably delightful rather than savagely critical. Poem 14 strikes the more casual note of the factory worker who drugs himself after work at the talkies or surreptitious love down by the canal, who dares do nothing for fear of the boss and of arbitrary unemployment without even a letter of recommendation. On the other hand there is the graduate of the public schools, splendid of face and Grecian of form. But the future does not love him; the future loves that miserable factory worker. Poem 17 rumbles with thunder coming over the Cotswolds. It accuses the seers of the past of not communicating the little vision of truth they had, of shading their statements and deliberately lying. No time has had greater advantages than the present. But, self-important, we assumed all of this sprang from us and we accepted it without thought. Thus the disciplined love which would have controlled the instruments of production was too difficult and too dull. Wilfred claimed that " 'the poetry is in the pity' " and Kathy desired in her journal " 'to be rooted in life.' " So there can be no excuse for idleness in the echo of these two ringing challenges; men and men's lives are changed not so much by what they contemplate as by what they do. The ultimate test of thought is always the action by which it issues into the objective world.

Poem 18 is a jolly little ditty about the sun shining on the ships at sea and also on you and me, but amidst barking dogs and growing crops the wind is blowing in a direction that most people do not discern. So everybody goes about his own business quite unaware that it is everybody's business when a judge enforces an obsolete law, a banker makes a war loan, an expert designs a long-range gun. Poem 20 gives a glimpse of the kind of love Auden both deplored and found general in his time, love which gave power but paralyzed the will to use that power. Poem 21 moves the same idea into the international scene with Hitler and Mussolini wooing confidence, Churchill acknowledging the greetings of a crowd, Roosevelt at the microphone, Van der Lubbe laughing. But love will do nothing on its own. We must plan, we must have convictions; only through our private lives can love perform its public function. Even love can be vassal to Fascist pretenses.

The second of two songs to Benjamin Britten claims that act should follow thought instantly, because that's what thought is for—to issue immediately into action. "Casino" begins with the habitués of gambling places to whom the rooms of play are temples of prayer, and the form of betting religious rites. But then, perhaps inexcusably, it leaps to the accusation of an entire generation, claiming that what was meant to be godlike will now never be born. Poem 27 returns to Auden's evolutionary theme. We are jealous of animals that act innocently and spontaneously and are gone; whereas we weep, feel duty, are carefully good, and eventually lose the things we love. Poem 28 is the social gospel's complaint against private love: the lovers make love on a bed in a railway terminus, entirely indifferent to all the other people sitting on their beds, watching with hostility. The trouble with love is not the relationship established, but the relationships denied.

Poem 30, to Christopher Isherwood, is another of the considerable poems in the volume. Auden is on August vacation by the sea, wishing Isherwood were there. Nine years before, on the Isle of Wight (where "wild Tennyson became a fossil"), they talked about the books they had read and the education they had received. Half boys, they still played the old games of spies, dark glasses, old felt hats (cf. "Argument" [*The Orators*]), but the game became guess and deduction about other visitors. Five summers later they watched the Baltic from a balcony. Now the radio roars out its warnings and lies, making both a decorous social life with others or private loneliness impossible. Everywhere they look they see virtue debased and vice exalted. In such an hour, Auden, in echo of his dedicatory phrase "narrow strictness," claims that the critical times require the "strict" and "adult" pen of such a writer as Isherwood who can warn us away from spurious colors and fake consolations, who can reveal the aridity of pretentious works and point out the squalor in the school and in the countryside. Not only can he give the critical insight that helps us resist fear and fight disaster, but more important, he can show us how we should act and help us to do it!

The epilogue, in characteristic Auden fashion, begins with a fragment of landscape, a city with cathedral, machinery, and dogs. The prophets of the time thunder, blackmail, betray, and terrify. Auden thinks of the prophets who gave understanding with patience and makes for himself a rosary of their names: Nansen, Schweitzer, Freud, Groddeck,

D. H. Lawrence, Kafka, Proust. But now hatred is triumphant and the gentle seers are dead; now power is in the hands of the hostile whose deepest desire is to wound. That's the way the world goes.

We have noted the importance of Spain to the whole group of poets. There men saw the nature of the antagonists and the shape of things to come for the whole world in the immediate future. So W. H. Auden in *Spain* (1937) says that, if you want to build the "just city," Spain is the place. If you wish to make a romantic suicide pact—the pitting of a few peasants against the massed machines and troops of dictators—this is the place. On that arid plain of Spain, a piece of Africa crudely soldered to the Europe of the industrial revolution, we can see our fears dramatized and played out by living actors. The menace becomes alive and precise.

Auden and Isherwood collaborated on another play, *On the Frontier* (1938), a melodrama in three acts. The setting is more political and international than in any of their other dramas, but the outcome is curiously individualistic, passive, and personal. Both sides of the frontier are sick; there is no health anywhere. The frontier runs down the stage midway between two families, but it is not the frontier between illness and health, inner and outer, or the old and new. It is a frontier of invincible hatred, prejudice, and fear—and horror lies on both sides. The frontier is crossed only by two young people. The crossing is made via a bridge of individual love, but issues only in a semireligious martyrdom and death. Thus the only two sane people in an insane world take refuge from the world in what they know to be an impossible love.

An abortive workers' revolution is staged at the Valerian Steel Trust of Westland, but it is betrayed from within as well as suppressed from without. At the center of the city there stands a great cathedral, but now the church is frequented only by peasants who have been in the city less than one generation and middle-class women who can't find husbands. The new center of the popular life is the Valerian Works. Man's fate is to work fast on the Valerian assembly line, eat lunch in the Valerian Cafeteria, make love in Valerian Park, buy the ring the next day at the Valerian store, settle down in a cosy Valerian villa, and educate dear children in patriotism and personal hygiene in the Valerian school. On weekends men may pop into their Valerian runabouts to picnic by a fake waterfall. If there are any savings they can be invested in the Valerian bank. Valerian doctors watch the health, and burial is from the Valerian funeral parlor—in other words, fully developed capitalism is exactly like complete state socialism. The arts and religion, even revolutionary clubs, will serve to sugarcoat the pill. Nature is not interested in the common people or in the remnants of aristocracy. It is interested only in the rich owners of the means of production and the rich suppliers of capital. However, it is wrong to assume that although there may be shooting in Russia and in Spain, it will never happen in Westland. A popular leader becomes the national martyr, but since he does all the suffering on behalf of the people, they can return to tea, whipped cream, and apple cakes.

As for the non-solution of interpersonal love, Eric and Anna (act 2, scene 1) have found a place where they may meet and be themselves, not Thorvalds or Vrodnys, not Westlanders and Ostnians, but young persons in love. But Eric goes to prison as a pacifist, and dying of a chest wound, is watched over by Anna, now a nurse, and also dying. Eric has no satisfaction even in his pacifism because he realizes that it is impossible to attempt to stand aside from the general madness. We are not free to choose our world, our era, or our class—for Auden, a significantly pessimistic admission.

Early in the summer of 1937, Auden and Isherwood were commissioned by Faber and Faber and by Random House to write a travel book about the East. The outbreak of the Sino-Japanese War in August made them decide to go to China. They left England January 1938 and returned at the end of July. For both this was their first journey to any spot east of Suez and they suffered the handicap of speaking no Chinese.

In a very interesting dedication to E. M. Forster, they examine their reasons for coming to China and their reactions once there. They discover that they are really very like Forster characters: excited by war, wishing to view catastrophe, they deny reason and ignore love. In Hong Kong they muse that they cannot blame the disorder of the world on a "general will"; they have only themselves to blame. England could stop the war, but will not, because she considers Japan a bastion against communism.

If *On the Frontier* is hopeless about the present and offers men no viable choices for the future, and *Journey to a War* shows the inevitability of an international landslide toward conflict, *In Time of War* (1939) represents Auden's earlier position when he assumed that man could still choose, and, although overshadowed by the coming catastrophe, there was still a little time to avert total collapse. A sonnet sequence with a verse commentary, the first twelve sonnets trace man's history (with special reference to China) from the expulsion from an oriental Garden of Eden (used as a symbol of innocence rather than as any specific religious dogma) to a corrupt world in which man must build a new environment by the application of his empirical findings. The first sonnet expresses one of Auden's favorite evolutionary views, that insects, fish, and fruit live by simple instinct, but man has all the possibilities of change, choice, of role-playing as leopard or dove, to search for truth, to make mistakes, to envy friends, and to choose his own love. Leaving Eden (sonnet 2) men found freedom wild and frightening. They exulted in the life of the senses (sonnet 3) as all things became alien and separate. They multiplied enormously and knew hatred, perverse love, and great oppression. One group of men (sonnet 4) decided to stay in the country, the life most like the Garden they had left. But staying, they were derided by townsmen, pitied by poets, or admired as the possessors of primal truth. The oppressors held them up as examples of the sheeplike character all men should have. The youthful radical who would set the young free (sonnet 5) became in his turn outdated, an upholder of law and order. Some fell in love with meditation upon truth (sonnet 6) but never served the truth with the deeds of their lives. Some became poets (sonnet 7) and expressed the gathered feelings of all the people. But when they ceased to express for the many and turned for inspiration to the domestic events of their own lives they lost their calling (cf. Day-Lewis's *From Feathers to Iron*). Some became democratic and capitalistic and the growth of their wealth choked out their lives (sonnet 8). The kingly and the saintly (sonnet 9) were revered, but their ideals did not move out into the lives of men. Sonnet 10 is a commentary on the life of a modern Christ. As a boy in the Temple, he was adored by the wisest. The poor sacrificed for his cause and martyrs brought him their lives to spend. But the needs of work and bed were pressing and so men built him a temple for worship and went about their business. So he slipped out of the temple to work by their sides and talk with them like a neighbor. And his temple became a place of fear and greed, the citadel of the tyrant and the tormentor of the martyrs. Sonnet 11 is a commentary on the life of David. God looks down on the humble shepherd who likes music. He proposed a dovelike mission for him, but David chose the eagle instead and learned new ways of killing—a political rather than a social career.

Sonnet 12 is a political parable based on the tale of Jack the Giant Killer. The people assume the giant to be dead and they relax. Poets, artists, and magicians are unhappy about the change, but the giant is delighted to have become invisible, for when he was visible he could be vanquished, now, unacknowledged, he conquers. The Demon in *The Ascent of F6* could not be killed, the Abbot said. To imagine so was the most serious of perfectionist delusions. Instead he could only be controlled and limited by eternal vigilance.

Sonnet 15 stresses again the importance of choice: it is possible at any time for a people to choose to turn away from freedom and to become luxuriously helpless like the rich, or penuriously helpless like the poor. Sonnets 25 and 27 sum up the matter succinctly. Our life is not predetermined like the animals; we have to find our own way by experimentation. Those who long for perfect order or who feel nostalgia for the old ways are hindrances to the coming of the new. A balance between the humble recognition of man's limitations and the proud recognition of his sovereign power to choose will show us the meaning of living in "freedom by necessity."

In 1939, the publication year of *In Time of War*, David Daiches considered Auden to be at a standstill (cf. reviews of MacNeice at the same period) because he was catching his breath after the decisive jump over to America. Although the poetry was technically excellent and maintained the high standards of intellectuality and vigor, the themes were generally those which had been indicated even if not entirely explored in the past. But a major change in Auden's ideology, not always recognized by the critics, was the shift to a Kierkegaardian frame of reference in the poet's definition of the nature of man, the possibilities of his relationship to other men, and the exigency of his relationship to God. Thus temporarily disregarding Auden's more habitual themes and manner of treatment, we shall concentrate our attention on the neo-orthodoxy of the poet as evidenced by *Another Time* and fully revealed in *New Year Letter*.

Perhaps the most remarkable thing about the format of *Another Time* (1940) is the number of poems that are about historic and contemporary persons and places. Historically, there are poems on A. E. Housman, Edward Lear, Rimbaud, Melville, Pascal, Voltaire at Ferney, Orpheus, Napoleon, and Matthew Arnold. Contemporaneously there are poems to the Novelist, the Composer, four cabaret songs for Hedli Anderson (second wife of Louis MacNeice), three elegies for W. B. Yeats, Ernst Toller, and Sigmund Freud. In terms of place, there are poems on Oxford, Brussels, Washington, D.C., Musée des Beaux Arts, Gare du Midi, Dover, Spain 1937. This accounts for twenty-two poems out of forty-five, or half of the book.

A pleasant occasional poem on Oxford is thoroughly neo-orthodox in its estimate of the condition of man. In the thoughtless natural world, the natural man knows Eros and thus must mingle hostility with his every love. The natural woman knows only Nature and thus can only love herself.

The eighth poem is a fast-moving ditty of trochaic tetrameter quatrains. But in the midst of its rhythmic insouciance we discover that the immortality of the Demon of F6 and of Jack the Killer's giant has now become the doctrine of the eternality of the Devil. The young hero perfectionist thinks to slay the Devil, to open the graves and rescue all those who fell into Satan's power, and to empty the earth of mortal sin. But the outcome is not the predicted death of the Devil, but the predictable death of the hero. A very serious little poem about Hell (poem 12) raises the questions of its existence and location. Perhaps it would be easiest if Hell were real and here, because then evil would be the natural state of existence; man would have no moral choices to make and he could not be expected to achieve any moral acts.

In an exciting poem about Herman Melville, good and evil are shown in constant Zoroastrian struggle right here in this world: evil shares our bed, eats at our table; we meet goodness every day. Good is strong and evil is helpless, but both are destroyed equally before our eyes (*Billy Budd*). It is only in the fantasy of dreams that we can imagine that anyone is spared from suffering and pain. Although the ways of God are past understanding (the equal destruction of both good and evil), the movement of human history is always within God's hand. If we quail before punishment, it turns out to be a "form of love"; if we fear the howling storm, it happens that we were sheltered in the Father's breast (*Moby Dick*). So like the secular existentialists, we learn to accept human vanity and to live with absurdity in such a way that they become the "calm [acceptance] of mountains." Thus religious or Kierkegaardian existentialism differs from the attitudes of Sartre and Camus because although there may be nausea at the discrepancy between this world and God's world, and revolt at the difference between the actual and the ideal, the outcome is neither tragic nor pathetic. If we can take the great leap that this is the absurd paradox of man's condition, then tragedy and pathos give way to comedy as man serenely accepts God's conditions and the limitations of his own existence.

In a poem on Pascal, the French thinker reverts to a

childhood nightmare in which he became aware that none of the relatives who should have loved him actually cared about him at all. Each was a single rose not daring to leave its self-regard for a moment. Thus in an alien world, looking up into a darkness that made no promises, he prayed a prayer that fell away into the abyss before and the abyss behind and was mocked by the unbelief of everyone around him. This is Kierkegaardian tragedy at its most intense, when the fearful and trembling soul can draw no comfort from human love and finds that even his faith in the Divine love has been infected and weakened by human infidelity.

A love song makes the only affirmation the neo-orthodox can make: the beloved is mortal, guilty of natural depravity, but entirely beautiful to the lover. Poem 30 is almost a dissenting voice from the past intruding into a new mood. We must live in today, yet many say "Not Now," and many have no discernible identity so that they cannot even say "I Am." If possible they would like to be lost in history. "Another Time" (the title poem of the book) will have other lives to live, therefore we must live in our own present.

The poem for September 1, 1939, describes the condition of natural depravity as born in the bones of every man. He wants the one thing he cannot have. Rejecting God's universal love, he demands to be loved for himself alone. But the poet asks that the "just" man (St. Paul's doctrine of justification), made of the same elements of self-seeking love and dust, may yet show an "affirming flame."

New Year Letter, dedicated to Elizabeth Mayer, January 1, 1940, represents for W. H. Auden the full shift from psychological analysis and political solutions to theology (instead of that empirical philosophy which had previously bound the group of poets together) and revealed religion. In 1939, with *The Still Centre*, it might be assumed that Stephen Spender was returning to some theory of individual salvation. In *Word Over All* (1942) Day-Lewis celebrates the single individual and his personal loves. In *Springboard* (1945) the most important of Louis Mac-

Neice's poems is one called "The Kingdom," and it is perhaps the ultimate expression of MacNeice's thought and
genius. The Kingdom seems to be composed of those rugged
individuals who, because they dared to be themselves in a
recalcitrant world, give hope and courage to others to do
likewise. This humanistic Kingdom exalts the anarchic
qualities of the unique individual and claims that its highest aim is the fullest realization of those qualities. Perhaps
because the message is unexpectedly affirmative rather than
negative, earnest rather than casual, the tone of the diction
is decidedly quiet and flat, almost with the diffidence of a
young man making his maiden avowal of faith. Underneath
the bureaucratic crust of society, claims the poet, there
exists a kingdom of individuals, equal in difference, separately sovereign. There is the candid scholar, the unselfish
priest, the uncomplaining mother, active men who manage
to be kind, generous contemplatives, happy-go-lucky saints,
peace-loving buccaneers. They are the vindications of the
human species, and they can be found everywhere.

Part 1 of Auden's poetic epistle is set in Brussels, 1939,
when everyone seems to have been manufacturing hopes to
avoid the certain sense of coming disaster. Then, the scene
moves to a cottage on Long Island while friends play
Buxtehude's passacaglia, and war engulfed Poland.

Eros and Apollo (stanza 4) desire order and will it to be,
but somehow they always produce its opposite. The great
masters of art always test desire by its result. To dreams,
they say "Deeds." To striving, "Succeed." To mourning,
"Forgive." To becoming, "Live." Dante, William Blake,
Rimbaud, Dryden, Catullus, Tennyson, Baudelaire, Hardy,
Rilke, and Kipling (stanza 5) are each epitomized by the
poet.

The situation of our time provides the setting of a
baffling crime. There lies the body which we all detested,
and all are suspects and involved (cf. Dostoevski, *The
Brothers Karamazov*). The more we look, with all our
equipment for criticism, the more the guilt spreads; it becomes a vast spiritual disorder everywhere under the sky.
The last decade (the 1930s) was so full of pain and despair

in Asia, Spain, Abyssinia, along the Danube, Germany and Poland that even men of good will are tempted to desire revenge (stanza 5).

In part 2 the decade ends and strangers, enemies, friends all find it hard to set aside pride, to learn who we are, to accept our limitations and inadequacies as men. Even Mephistopheles is only Creation's errand boy and often ends by driving us toward good ends. Having no real existence of his own, he comes into being from the fear, faithlessness, and hatred of men. His passion is to damn; his proper place is to "push us into grace" (stanza 3). The best protection against his wiles is to remember that we live in eternity. The devil is the great splitter of creation. But if reality be dual, then what happens to a God half of whose creation is not his? And if monistic, then of what use is it for the Devil to fight?

Some dreamed the Communists were a higher species, the potential man. They visualized Karl Marx in the British Museum reading room writing: "None shall receive unless they give," thus enunciating the dogma that cooperation is the law of life. We all hoped and waited for the day that the state would wither away, expecting the millennium. But it didn't come; freedom is still far from home. Moscow is just as foreign as Rome or Paris (stanzas 9–12).

It is New Year's Eve in part 3, and across the East River from Elizabeth's house Manhattan blazes with lights. A week earlier the poet had attended a wedding dinner at which Schubert, Mozart, and Gluck were played. The music, food, and friendship produced the "real republic" (stanza 2), that state that all politicians, even the worst, claim as their aim. Every day produces some such bright brief revelation of the shining center of life to every person. That magnetic spot (cf. Day-Lewis's use of "magnetic") cannot be arranged or scheduled; it may be defined as "free rejoicing energy" (stanza 3); it comes casually, anytime, accidentally. It is Being without any pain of Becoming in a state of Eternal Innocence. But the Perfect Being has ordained that this moment must be quickly lost in order to be quickly regained. If a man attempts to stay always eating of the tree in the orchard, Paradise becomes Hell.

Then follows a significant definition of man's nature—he is separate from God and other men in will, freedom, and the power of self-completion. His cardinal sin is to claim for Becoming the qualities of Being. His Hell is the result of the lie that Becoming and Being are the same and thus he turns away from suffering. We can bear suffering; what we cannot bear is the intolerable fear that we add ourselves, certainly we cannot "will" Heaven, but neither do we have to will Hell; we can will Purgatory instead. Time is the area in which we must and do sin; this is the life we live three quarters of the time (T. S. Eliot, *The Cocktail Party*); it is the purgatorial hill which we must climb (Eliot, *The Family Reunion*) even though we know that once achieved we will see a higher ridge on the other side (a more expansive and pioneering use of the myth of Sisyphus than Camus's). This is the very game for which we have natural skill, and besides it's good for the production of muscles (the orthodox doctrine of the necessity of temptation and sin in order to strengthen our faith). And when we wake up from our dreams of glory, we must not be dejected to find ourselves still in Purgatory, rather than citizens of the Kingdom of God. We are sufficiently earthbound that, if the truth were told, we are a little relieved still to have our feet firmly on the damp earth. This is where we belong, where everyone and everything sins, and we can be half angel, half *petite bête*. So, perched on a sharp edge of rock, whence if we do not move we fall, faith balanced by doubt, admitting that probably every route we choose is the wrong one, we believe that each time we climb a little higher, we ascend a penitential trail that forces us to remain free with free wills. Recognizing all this, the state of our mind becomes "reverent frivolity" (stanza 5).

How does one choose his way? He must not yield to little human particles who claim to have all truth, nor follow raving demagogues, nor blindly worship the state. The issues are very great and quite different from any previous time. This is not Rome falling to Vandal, Goth, and Hun. They had the pure instinctive joy in destruction that animals have, but we are refined creatures of machine and mind (stanza 6).

There are two domains: the public marketplace where acts are done which are common to all men. There each man must choose his vocation, domicile, and life-style. The other domain is inner, private, the landscape of will and need. But even if a man considers this inner landscape to be Hellish, this is a landscape against which he may not rebel (Lucifer), and from which he may not escape ("Paid On Both Sides"). Do not make the mistake of Edmund Burke and think these spheres are the same; in the first sphere every man is a brother; in the second each man is a king (stanza 7).

Out of the Renaissance and the Reformation a new anthropos has emerged: empiric, economic, urban, prudent, inventive, with profit as his incentive and work as the meaning of his public life. Rousseau, Blake, Kierkegaard, and Baudelaire were all prophets crying that this development was moving in the wrong direction. The mass ignored them, but they were right and the mass was wrong. His job, his goods, his pleasures took charge of man instead of the exercise of his freedom. This ended up in a world of the privileged on one side of the track, and the disregarded on the wrong side, with hatred in between. We blame the political leaders for the situation, but we ourselves share the blame and guilt. The politician is nothing but the average of the populace. Liberty becomes the freedom to achieve separate privilege, rather than a sharing of blessing (stanzas 13–16).

It is getting late and the bars are closing for the night. The revelers will once again become tightened selves, thus able to walk safely through the irritations of the next day. America is a land of nomads, manufacturers moving to the south, Okies to the west coast, Negroes to the northern cities—all commuters instead of pioneers. But each individual senses that each one is alone and alien (stanzas 18–19).

Alas, goodness is never so easy to achieve or so plain to see as evil. We will awaken on New Year's Day to a fearful world. One thing we can always say: true democracy begins with the free confession by all of all of our sins. Yet real unity begins with the recognition of difference: each has his own needs to satisfy, each his own power to supply (stanzas 20–21).

The letter closes with a petition to Unicorn, Dove, Ichthus, Wind, Voice, Clock, Keeper, Source. We need help to lose carelessness and coldness; we need to be instructed in the civil arts of building a city that will have a sense of locality and will enjoy peace. Let there be sufficient strength for this in our day. The benediction is in the form of a pleasant personal greeting to Elizabeth. A dear friend who forgives, she helps when we fall down dancing and smiles when we make the same old ridiculous mistakes (stanzas 22–23).

5

From Romantic Revolution to Welfare State

Three eras in literary history have served as points of reference and comparison in this study of four contemporary British poets. The first era falls in the early 1800s when Napoleon Bonaparte was being metamorphized from the Protector of the People into the Emperor of the French, the conqueror of much of Europe, and part of Africa. At the beginning of the French Revolution, William Wordsworth exclaimed: "Bliss was it in that dawn to be alive, / But to be young was very Heaven!" He was overjoyed that Reason was moving out of the mind into "the very world, which is the world / Of all of us,—the place where, in the end, / We find our happiness, or not at all!" At the end, he mourned that France had shifted from self-defense to conquest: "But now, become oppressors in their turn, / Frenchmen had changed a war of self-defence / For one of conquest, losing sight of all / Which they had struggled for." In the course of events, it seemed to Wordsworth that England herself had played the role of oppressor: "with open war / Britain opposed the liberties of France." [1]

In the Argument of "France: An Ode," Samuel Taylor Coleridge wrote: "still the Poet struggled to retain the hope that France would make conquests by no other means than by presenting to the observation of Europe a people more happy and better instructed than under other forms of Government."

George Gordon, Lord Byron, lamented Napoleon's fall at Waterloo: "In 'pride of place' here last the eagle flew," [2] and in "The Masque of Anarchy," Percy Bysshe Shelley wrote about the rise of liberty in France, the gathering of neighbor nations to quench its flame, but the complete powerlessness of all tyrants, whether in France or abroad, to extinguish that flame.

Corresponding societies with French Jacobins sprang up all over England. The Romantic philosopher William Godwin at first seemed too tepid in his enthusiasm for the grand French experiment to make liberty, equality, and fraternity come down out of the arcane of idealism to preside over the daily affairs of men and of nations. Less than a decade later the same philosopher was considered so dangerous a radical that he had to turn to the writing of history texts for children, written under a pseudonym, published by his wife. If Godwin had maintained a fatal consistency it was the British liberals who blew first hot and then cold, who saw the execution of Louis XVI as a threat to the English monarchy, who viewed the English Channel as a frail protection against French invasion, who placed cairns of wood on the coastal cliffs to be fired in warning of a French landing, who, in a frenzy of backlash, reestablished the licensing and censorship of the publication of books and the production of plays. So the popular hero became the universal villain and the poetic hopes for a new era in the lives of men waned and guttered out.[3]

The second point of reference is the proletarian poets of the 1930s. In the decade 1930–40, Day-Lewis, Spender, MacNeice, and Auden addressed their poetry to two burning questions—what is wrong with England, and what can be done about it?

Cecil Day-Lewis, youthful rebel and later Poet Laureate of England, schoolmaster, and writer of detective fiction under the pseudonym Nicholas Blake, considered that the writer in England, circa 1930, was living in a sick society. Amid rusting iron-works and abandoned mines (stanza 33, *Transitional Poem* [1929]) he takes a light-engine back along the tracks to make inventory of the moribund past (*The Magnetic Mountain* [1933]). A Socialist Christ, he calls Britons to leave all this and join the pilgrimage to the magnetic mountain.

In the year 1938, he insists that liberal individualism is

powerless in the contemporary condition of the world. The liberal mind cannot seem to grasp that its era of opportunity has passed (*Starting Point*) and that the encrusted conditions of man's life can be changed only by radical breakthrough. In *Overtures to Death and Other Poems* (1938), he totally rejects the outmoded idea that society can be recreated and regenerated by merely individual acts of goodness.

An unsatisfied dualist from the beginning, he expressed that dividedness philosophically by the tensions between ideas of abstract beauty versus the loveliness of one particular maiden (*Beechen Vigil* [1925]; "Cyprian, Cyprian!" *Country Comets* [1928]) and existentially between idea and actuality. In "It Is the True Star" (*Country Comets*), he demands that every idea and program must submit to the testing of the objective world. In part 1 of *Transitional Poem*, he claims that it is only the human brain that has the power to stamp order upon the disorder of life. And in "Between Hush and Hush" he embraces things so ardently that all seems ready for the introduction of Marxian materialism.

Although he tends to say less about politics than Spender and Auden, in that little he is by far the most explicit and dedicated. As a constitutional dualist he loves the past but finds only the future to be electric and creative ("Johnny Head-In-Air," *Transitional Poem*, extended in *A Time to Dance* [1935], discussed in *A Hope for Poetry* [1934]. Despite his personal predilection he is convinced that in his era the poet must become a propagandist for the new world. Convinced that socialism offers the only hope for western man, yet he accepts that help reluctantly and has to keep convincing himself of its necessity ("The Conflict," *A Time to Dance*).

He struggles to remember that all his privileged life he has been borne aloft on the shoulders of the underprivileged ("Moving In," *A Time to Dance*). When Anthony Neale finally finds a *Starting Point* for a contemporary, useful life at the end of the novel, that point is total dedication to the workers' cause.

Those who succeed on the pilgrimage to the new world,

will, paradoxically, be men of committed position. Even more paradoxically the reluctant dualist prays that his coming child (*From Feathers to Iron* [1931]) may be either the complete conformist, happily unthinking about his societally imposed role, or an utter rebel so full of conviction that he has no need of props from the opinions of others.

Day-Lewis's commitment to communism began with the stirring admonition to poets to relate to the coming revolution, moved on to describe that revolution's Utopian aspects, and spluttered out in generalized concern for humanity. A poet is only a dope-peddler unless he joins the class revolution ("Johnny Head-In-Air," *A Time to Dance*). When the stern demands for disciplined self-sacrifice of the world class war is over, then man may enjoy personal pleasure in a period of the withering-away of government (poem 31, *The Magnetic Mountain*), cf. Auden, *New Year Letter*, part 2, stanza 11. When Noah's flood of the masses is past and the waves of workers have receded, the raven of tenderness and the dove of peace will emerge from the ark and the wedding of waves and hills will bring forth a new and nobler race of men (*Noah* [1936]). But by the end of the decade, causes, even the most hopeful of them, have waned and only humanity persists in the double forms of problem and potential. It is too late to warn, too early to hope; war has obliterated all human relationship but sympathy (part 1, *Word Over All* [1945]).

The waning commitment is all the more pathetic in view of the poet's earlier high hopes for the coming revolution. *The Magnetic Mountain* of communism had attractive power that no simple change of environment could provide. Out of a world going up in flames the comrades of the new movement went swinging along, more united in heart than in head. A bourgeois writer, like Noah (*Noah*) he sees the threat of the coming workers' revolution earlier than others. But, ark all built with enthusiasm and hope, he finds the workers' revolution which was going to bring world peace jostled aside by a world war against fascism fomented by incipiently Fascist capitalists. So his Utopian vision of world peace and brotherhood is punctured by the bitter urgencies of another world war (*Overtures to Death and Other Poems*) and his message wanes with the dimming vision into simple compassion for sufferers.

Stephen Spender also faced the question: what is wrong with England? He answered that England had lost all positive belief (*The Destructive Element* [1935]). Its symptoms are obvious: the cities decay, the factories lie idle or undermanned, a large percentage of the nation's manpower is unemployed (*Trial of a Judge* [1938]), power is controlled by corrupt and inept politicians (canto 2, *Vienna* [1934]), and aristocrats pride themselves on their own stupidity ("The Cousins" [1936]). Even the most enlightened leadership is distracted and uncertain ("Exiles from Their Land, History Their Domicile," *The Still Centre* [1939]).

In the modern industrial society, a prisoner in a jail has actually been a prisoner all his life—of slum, genetics, race, class, poverty, and exploitation by the upper classes ("The Prisoners," *The Still Centre*). Individual illness is a fractured segment of the vast malaise of the age. The heroine of "The Dead Island" (1936) is a victim of drink, drugs, sex, cafe society—the anodynes of industrial pain—and the final loss of her cash—the unforgiveable sin in a capitalistic culture.

Much of Spender's understanding of England's illness comes from his school-boy memories. What a difference between what his home life had led him to expect and what he actually found in the world ("What I Expected," *The Still Centre*)! Delicate, idealistic, of mixed Jewish-Gentile ancestry (*Trial of a Judge*; "The Cousins), Stephen found the experience of boarding school utterly hellish. Through the semifictitious hero Geoffrey Brand, he gives us a searing picture of British preparatory school, corrosive enough to match Dickens's *Oliver Twist*.

Yet, the lonely school boy later insists that "An 'I' Can Never Be Great Man" (*Poems*), and counsels his liberal friends to accept the methodology of communism because it is the only contemporary force with the confidence of belief and the sureness of operation requisite to defeat fascism (*Forward from Liberalism*). The vague good will of liberalism he considers to be of no value in dealing with the positive evil of nazism (*Trial of a Judge*).

Spender participates in that shift from the ideal to the actual so important to the poetry of his era. In "Acts Passed Beyond the Boundary of Mere Wishing" (*Poems*), he demands that love shall be so palpable that it can provide electric power to light a whole city. In "The Express" (*Poems*), he claims that a fast train is more relevant to the lives of modern men than any concept of God or Nature. He considers the human body to be less efficient than an airplane ("Variations on My Life—the First," *The Still Centre*). Quoting from Joseph Conrad and Henry James, he insists that although outside reality is dangerous to intellectuals and idealists, it is the test of a truly relevant, revolutionary art (*The Destructive Element*).

Therefore poetry in the 1930s must take account of politics and economics. He considered that all the advanced writers of his day were in revolt against the imitation in literature of middle-class life and thought (*The New Realism* [1939]). In the new and increasing dialogue between what Disraeli called "the two nations," Spender saw himself as an autobiographer endlessly seeking forms to express the stages of his own personal development.

Spender rejected the preceding poetic movements as unrelated to the present hour: the Georgian poets did not sustain the shock of war; the war poets, 1914–18, either died in the war or their talents were numbed by the shock, the 1920s poets were despairing, cynical, effete, and nonpolitical. Only in the 1930s did poets begin to return to the real world of fact and the consideration of their places in politics and society as well as culture.

He was quick to admit that a Communist writer is judged only on his dialectical orthodoxy and that the censorship of topics upon which one may write is intolerable, but he adds that the artist who remains uninvolved in the coming revolution has the greater problem of irrelevancy (*The Still Centre*). He agrees that relevance depends upon the degree of identification with the working class but he cannot accept the dogmatic dismissal of all non-Communist writers as having nothing to say worth the hearing (*The New Realism*).

Spender clearly looked forward to a day when a working-class reading audience would create cultural patterns of their own. He wrote the eulogy of a worker in a safety-belt factory ("The Funeral," *Collected Poems: 1928–1953*), and idolized Petra's dying brother because his life and death had counted for the workers' cause (*Trial of a Judge*). In both *Vienna* (1934) and *Returning to Vienna* (1947) he made much of a Socialist hero and martyr, describing living workers as the supporters of the future world, and dead workers as if they were fallen angels. He was convinced that in the class war the workers would win both because of the basic nature of their occupations and their vast numerical superiority (*Trial of a Judge*).

In his personal and his political life, Spender had always been much concerned with the proper relation of one individual to other individuals (*World Within World*), and of one individual to social groups ("My Parents Kept Me from Children Who Were Rough," *Poems*). Perhaps for this very reason he demanded that other writers address their attention to the central social-political problem of his time. Out of this concern came mutually opposing convictions. First he felt that the late 1920s heard the last gasp of the idea that an individual, simply by accepting his own personal responsibility and without uniting with some larger group, could influence history (*Forward from Liberalism*). Yet, second, by the end of the 1930s he was reluctant to be forced to choose between East and West, socialism and capitalism, Russia and America (*World Within World*). He simply wanted the freedom to be and to express himself. Of course this came at a time when he recognized that the exploited could become fatal tyrants in their turn (*The Backward Son*), that the discipline of any expanding state—Capitalist, Socialist, or Fascist—tends to crush the individual gaiety of children ("The Bombed Happiness," *The Still Centre*). The thought of millions of Asiatic or semi-Asiatic minds totally without individual color filled him with horror (*Trial of a Judge*).

From his earliest collection of poems, *Blind Fireworks*

(1929) Louis MacNeice saw himself as a poet-prophet who lived in a sick society. In "Eclogue for Christmas" (*Poems* [1935]), he called it a diabetic culture, subsisting on sweets and ready at any moment to go into insulin shock. In "Neurotics," he compares Aeneas' successful flight from burning Troy to modern men who will perish along with their moribund culture. The "Eclogue" portrays men in the city as splintered, abstracted, irretrievably trivial. But men in the country are no better. The people who run the nation are bailiffs in a country being swallowed by debt, psychiatrists who can analyze but not cure, ministers of peace who function in the direction of war, movie actresses who become the sex symbols for a whole generation, and venal politicians easily bought.

Instead of self-examination to discover the sources of infection, the official and the influential project their failure outward in a frantic terror of bolshevism (*Roundabout Way* [1932]). But the real problem is the failure of liberalism. In "The Wolves" (*Poems* [1935]), while the Fascist enemies of freedom howl from the mainland the liberal men of good will join hands, build little sand castles on the beach, and try to shut out the howls of menace by increased talk and laughter. Chamberlain sells Czechoslovakia to the enemy, saving British skins but losing British souls.

The gentle hedonism propagated by liberalism is too delicate a plant to survive a class war. *The Last Ditch* (1940) portrays the ex-liberal with his back against a wall of self-imposed limitations. The poet toasts a Communist ("To a Communist," *Poems*), but questions the long-range goals of communism. To his friends he accuses Communist ideology of being puritanical—Sunday school treats and Esperanto. In "Hidden Ice" (*The Earth Compels* [1938]), he warns that trying to be an active Communist could destroy everything else a man wanted to preserve.

That some form of socialism is due cannot be be denied ("Coal and Fire," *Blind Fireworks*); it is the next inevitable form of the Industrial Revolution. But overshadowing its coming loom two great dreads. The first is the sure coming of war. When MacNeice attempts to write a morning song

("Aubade," *Poems*), it is interrupted by newsboys crying war. Without too much of a tremor he mentions the fall of Seville in the "Epilogue for W. H. Auden" (*Letters from Iceland*); by the sixth canto of *Autumn Journal* he admits that Seville has followed him to London. Sitting in his pleasant apartment on Hampstead Heath, drinking the health of his friend Wystan Auden, at any moment there may be the rap of a gun-butt at the door ending all civilian comforts and freedoms.

The second dread is more dire than even the threat of war. From his earliest writing the rectory child has felt that all mankind is under a sentence. The sun turns dark ("Morning Sun," *Poems*), the fountain sprays ashes, Perseus whirls away forever transfixed by the dread Medusa ("Perseus," *Poems*), the time-god Prometheus is ready at a moment to become the hammer-god Thor to smash everything into utter annihilation. The boiling sulphur basins of Iceland become emblems of the tortures of Hell, and London itself will sometime join the annihilation of Babylon, Nineveh, and Troy.

In the characteristic MacNeice manner the emblems of doom appear in the most lighthearted poems with the most insouciant melodies. Amidst the pleasant chitchat with an attractive woman in a bar ("Homage to Clichés," *The Earth Compels*), the imagery turns from the twinkling tails of tiny fish to a black panther to eight black bells in a womb of stone. We reassured ourselves that they were meant to be chimed; we really knew that such bells could only be tolled.

W. H. Auden, from private-school-days on the dominant member of the proletarian poets, also diagnosed the illness of England, but with significant differences. He moves rapidly from the delineation of clogged harbors and run-down factories where society is preparing its own grave (*Poems* [1930]), to the crimes of the upper and middle classes which have produced this impasse (*The Orators* [1932]). A culture should honor health and dishonor sickness, but his culture does just the opposite (Dedication, *Poems*). The mere existence of a healthy man becomes a rebuke to a sick society and it must find some way to infect or remove him (*Poems*).

Although his age is strong on diagnosis and weak on prescription, Auden feels that he knows the exact center and dimension of the disease. All illness is a manifestation of the death wish and society is engaged in *The Dance of Death* (1933). Our basic problem is the refusal to change (poem 3, *Poems*). The pillars of society, from this point of view, are signs of decay, not strength, because their rigidity points toward the past and death. Because the past is hopelessly tainted by old treacheries ("Paid on Both Sides," *Poems*), we must cut ourselves ruthlessly from that past. In a sick society, even love is sick and has lost its power to heal ("Paid on Both Sides"). The press provides only an anodyne to drug the public into acceptance of their unfulfilled, unheroic lives (*The Ascent of F6* [1936]). Dissatisfied with the decay of liberalism and afraid of the strength of communism we are likely to become Fascists, adoring the hero who is not afraid to wield power to preserve the old world (*The Orators*). The life force (Man-Woman, "Paid on Both Sides") has treated us in the past as favorites. But if we so resolutely choose death, it must find some other avenue of operation.

Unlike the members of the Auden group, Auden himself is never optimistic about state socialism as Utopia. Indeed he points out that fully developed capitalism is exactly like complete state socialism; simply substitute the word "Company" for "State" (*On the Frontier* [1938]). Nor is he so optimistic about the nature of man. The demon of the mountain can never be killed—this is a dangerous liberal notion—he is a continuing part of the life of every man and must be kept precariously within limits in each age (*The Ascent of F6*). Thus being neither idealist nor Communist, he can only describe himself as a "selfish pink old Liberal to the last" ("Letter to Lord Byron," *Letters from Iceland* [1937]).

In a way, Auden's movement from ideal to actual was more curious than that of other members of the group. Observation, dispassionate and uninvolved, was necessary to Auden as the clinical mood of diagnosis. But once diagnosis was complete, observation must be dropped summarily and action adopted. Auden seems never to have undergone any struggle about the liaison of poetry and politics. Emblems of power, authority, and group dynamic are to be found in his earliest poetry, albeit generally in the Fascist terms of utter devotion to a hero-leader and complete absorption of the individual in the elite group.

The idealization of the workers that was so prominent an element in the poetry of Spender and Day-Lewis is almost completely absent from the poetry of Auden. The nearest he comes is when Alan and Francis dissolve their upper-class ties to their middle-class town of Pressan Ambo and stride off to join the workers' revolution (*The Dog Beneath the Skin* [1935]). But like Edward Upward and Stephen Spender, an empty silence is preserved concerning what happens after they join.

In the isolation of his overwhelming cleverness, Auden gave much consideration to the nature and function of man. Whereas Spender and Day-Lewis were more concerned with their part in social groups, MacNeice and Auden assumed that if the proper identity of man were once established, appropriate relationships would then result. Thus when Auden contrasted a life of compromised action and dubious effect, in *The Ascent of F6*, with the life of contemplation and knowledge offered by the Abbot, he was attracted by the latter, not because it was an evasion of action but because the limitation of the power of evil (Demon) to the desert wastes of the world is a prime function of man.

Auden points out that man is not free to choose his world, his era, or his class (*On the Frontier*), but within certain well-defined limits he has the power to choose between alternatives (*The Ascent of F6*). In the face of the eternality of both God and the Devil (poem 8, *Another Time* [1940]), man is painfully aware of the ridiculousness of human vanity, the absurd nature of the world, and the consequent limitations upon man's freedom. The alternative to his painful awareness is the serene acceptance of the divine will by mountains and seas ("Herman Melville," *Another Time*).

The world is neither Eden nor Paradise; it is the setting

for a cosmic crime, and there lies the corpse for all to see. Everyone is by nature and opportunity under suspicion and the guilt of all is made clear by their distance from God and from each other. It is not within our power to will Heaven. We must not will Hell. But we can will Purgatory, the way-station where men have creative choices allied to the possibility of decisive movement (*New Year Letter*).

While Spender and Day-Lewis made their Socialist allegiance entirely clear and MacNeice agreed with socialism intellectually but not emotionally, Auden had little interest in the joining of parties. Indeed what occasionally resembles Marxian dialectic in his poetry could as well be his personal brand of philosophical materialism. He noted how easily the workers' revolution could be diverted by a clever demagogue into renewed nationalism (*The Dance of Death*). When he portrays an abortive workers' revolution, it is not only suppressed from above, but also betrayed from within (*On the Frontier*).

Nevertheless he is entirely Marxist in his insistence that when a culture has reached a certain state of rigidity, it cannot be renovated; it must be totally destroyed to make way for a new impulse (poems 28, 29, *Poems*). So violent death is a frequent feature in his early poems (*The Orators*) and to the bewildered question about the contemporary lack of leadership, he brusquely replied that the true leaders were not at home shoring up the remnants of Western culture. They were at "Cape Wrath" preparing for the coming world cataclysm (poem 24, *Poems*). Intellectuals must learn to accept the Communist abridgement of freedom as a temporary restriction which will finally result in great social benefit (poem 2, *Look, Stranger!* [1936]).

In "Spain" (1937), Auden had quickly recognized that the civil war in the Iberian peninsula was a kind of test-run for totalitarianism against the liberties of all free men everywhere. Earlier, writing to former students who were now in army camps, he warned that they were fighting to save a defunct capitalism of which the chief foe was the working class of their own nation (ode 5, *The Orators; The Dance of Death*). *In Time of War* (1939) could still warn men of the total collapse to come. But by 1938 and *Journey to a War* the inevitable landslide toward international war had already begun. Auden shared the other proletarian poets' keen sense that at that particular juncture in human history, war was a vast diversion forcing protest minorities back into national majorities, ending unemployment, turning the attention of the electorate from domestic to international problems, and making irrelevant social ideals which were on the verge of implementation. Thus the coming of revolution was to some measure blotted out by the coming of war, and the idealism that was meant to flame in world-changing event was cheapened into resurgent nationalism and a subsequent negation of ideals.

The third point of reference is established by the "angry young men" of England in the 1950s. When Jimmy Porter spouts defiance of education, religion, love, and government, and laments the absence of good causes, he matched the state of mind of literary Englishmen who were in their late twenties to middle thirties. "I suppose people of our generation aren't able to die for good causes any longer. . . . There aren't any good, brave causes left. If the big bang does come, and we all get killed off, it won't be in aid of the old-fashioned, grand design. It'll just be for the Brave New nothing-very-much-thank-you. About as pointless and inglorious as stepping in front of a bus." [4]

In the production of John Osborne's *Look Back In Anger*, London 1956, irritated intelligentsia found the symbol of their dissatisfaction. The term *angry young men* derives from the play and passed into the common coinage of speech to stand with the Lost Generation of the 1920s and the Bright Young Men of the 1930s. Although the group title is as angrily denied by the poets of the fifties as the Proletarian Poets, the Oxford Poets, or the Auden Group by the poets of the thirties,—it must be admitted that they are not angry in the usual sense, they are not all so very young, and they are not all men—yet they share a vigorous and predominantly negative viewpoint that made them the most important literary phenomenon of the 1950s. The four best known are novelists Kingsley Amis, John Wain, John

Braine, and playwright John Osborne. Other writers who share generally the same point of view include novelists Doris Lessing (*The Grass Is Singing*) and Iris Murdoch (*Under the Net*), as well as essayist Colin Wilson (*The Outsider*) and his close disciple Stuart Holroyd (*Emergence from Chaos*).

Although two of the number, Wilson and Holroyd, have been loosely accused of Fascist tendencies (cf. Auden's self-accusation in *The Orators*), the majority might be described as left-wing Socialists. When Amis was interviewed concerning his "program," if any, he said he'd start by nationalizing everything in sight. Then he would abolish the public schools, the aristocracy, and the House of Lords. Personally he would like to get rid of the royal family, except that the queen provided symbolic "sentimental glue" for the Commonwealth.

In a recent issue of *Encounter*, critic Frank Hilton produced a diagnosis of England's sickness strikingly like the illness theory of Auden, Isherwood, and Spender: "This country is sick, without confidence, neurotic. . . . [We are] sick of Britain, the Britain we're supposed to be, the first rate power that we're not, the great little island no one ever allows us to forget we once were, with our Agincourts and our Trafalgars and our gallant retreat from Dunkirk and all the crazy, bewildering, jingo junk we call our heritage."

But there are marked differences as well. The Bright Young Men of Oxford in the thirties were usually revolting against the "old school-tie," upper-class conservatism which they had inherited along with the family silver. Thus they tended to become gentlemen radicals, writing deep pink Marxist poetry in Georgian manor houses. They diagnosed the ills as Hilton did, but they prescribed a heart change which could arise only out of utter personal commitment. As John Wain commented; the proletarian poets had "a crushing sense, now extinct, of personal responsibility. It was the last age . . . in which people had the feeling that if they only took the trouble to *join* something, get a party card, . . . organize meetings and bellow slogans, they could influence the course of events."

For one thing, none of the AYM could honestly pose as upper-class writers. Osborne's mother was a barmaid; Wain's father was a dentist, but the playwright grew up near Manchester in the industrial "Five Towns" dominated by kilns and furnaces. Braine was the son of a city maintenance employee in the depressing Yorkshire town of Bradford. Amis's father was a minor office worker in London. Such men are not about to "join the working class"—they *are* workers. And they do not imagine that if you can find a worker he will escort you out of upper-class hypocrisy into a realistic workers' Utopia. They not only do not believe in Utopias, they don't believe in the Labour party or in very much of anything.

In the historical context, the Angry Young Men of the forties and fifties are as different from their predecessors, the Oxford Poets, as the latter were different from their eminent Edwardian predecessors. The Edwardians represented to both groups the Establishment, which, to the AYM included the institution of royalty. Thus John Osborne described the present members of the royal family as "the gold filling in a mouthful of decay" and the popular reverence for the royal family as "the national swill." But the significant point is that the proletarian poets voluntarily and individually broke away from the aristocratic ranks, whereas the Establishment represented to the Angry Young Men the people and institutions which kept new talents from receiving all the admiration and power they felt they deserved.

Historically the process seems to have gone something like this. The revolution the proletarian poets feared, prophesied, and demanded was overwhelmed by the Second World War—at just about the point that the poet-prophets had lost their vision and were no longer so sure of the direction of the promised land. But the postwar Labour government of 1945–51 fulfilled many particular goals of the revolution that had not arrived; a tax structure to absorb hereditary wealth, educational opportunities for bright youth regardless of parentage and class, the gigantic apparatus of social welfare (socialized medicine, unemployment compensation, etc.) spawned by Labourites but later pledged by Conservatives.

The welfare state which showered humane blessing also withered up the challenge and excitement of the Edwardian world. The oppressive income tax to support humanitarianism took away so much salary incentive that young people were handed over to an era of mediocrity: never starve, never get comfortable, a second-hand car in the garage, and an installment-plan television set in the parlor.

So the flavor of the welfare state revolution is oddly flat, productive of more disgruntlement, irritation, and cynicism than angry protest. If the AYM were enemies of gentility, they also hated bohemianism—precious or pretentious writing, experimentation in style and effect. Turning away from the metaphysics of Kafka, Joyce, Cocteau, Faulkner, Kingsley Amis substitutes his own existential question: " 'How am I going to pay the electric bill?' "

Sensing that England was suffering from an unacknowledged malaise, the proletarian poets diagnosed, shuddered, and prescribed socialism. With all the power that poetry adds to prose statement, they proposed pilgrimages to magnetic mountains, ideal friendships, and utter confidence in the workers' cause. They demanded that the upper-class intelligentsia become politically responsible and insisted that art be subservient to social necessities. Unfortunately but inevitably they linked their faith in a Communist revolution with the Socialist experiment being conducted in Russia. When, with the Berlin-Moscow Nonaggression Pact of 1939, they discovered that a Communist power was subject to exactly the same international political exigencies as any Capitalist country, they faced a multifaceted dilemma. Their original diagnosis remained firm—the patient was ill. But the prescription no longer commanded confidence and the prognosis became fuzzy, diverse, or faded into regretful silence.

The Angry Young Men of the fifties had inherited the postwar social benefits and still remained disenchanted. Skeptical of all political activity and commitment, they seem to have returned to the individualistic theory of doing the best possible by the exercise of their own personal talents—separately and politically unaligned—the very position of his predecessors that MacNeice had inveighed against in *Autumn Journal*. They vote Labour only because the Tories are worse: with inverse snobbishness they accept Amis's sour description of Labour party leadership: "those bloated career trade union leaders and those frightful little men, those Public School socialists." The two groups of writers agree on one basic fact—the loss of England's world leadership. Prophesied by the proletarians as evil omens, it was suffered in actual experience by the AYM as they became the unwilling and disgusted "chroniclers of Britain's shrinking-pains."

As, in the passage of time, the thirties' poets and the Angry Young Men of the fifties became contemporaries, it is interesting to note the directions their individual destinies took. C. Day-Lewis, in an article written for the New York *Times* on the one hundredth anniversary of the death of William Wordsworth, remarked that as a man who once had been beguiled by the Utopian hope of communism and later disillusioned by the political form it took in the Soviet Republic, he was well equipped to understand an earlier writer who had at first been attracted by the French Revolution then later repelled by it. So Day-Lewis began as a poet of such revolutionary fervor that he could parody Wordsworth's stirring lines: "Milton, thou shouldest be living at this hour / England hath need of thee," by substituting Lenin for Milton, and then became Poet Laureate himself in 1968.

After alienating the trustees of Cheltenham College where he taught from 1930 to 1935, he resigned even though C. M. Bowra had intervened on the young radical's behalf. He wrote his first detective novel in 1935 to raise one hundred pounds for the repair of the stone-tiled roof of his cottage. Thereafter, under the *nom de plume* Nicholas Blake, he wrote more than twenty mystery novels which John Buchan, along with the general public, seems to have preferred to his widely read verse. In *Wind Over All* (1943) he reverted to his native gift for the short lyric and traditional forms of diction and imagery. He translated Virgil's *Aeneid* and retold Greek myths in *Pegasus and Other Poems*. Professor of Poetry at Oxford, 1951–56, and Norton Professor of Poetry at Harvard, 1964–65, he joined the London Ministry of Information during the war years and later became a director of the publishers Chatto and Windus.

After his second marriage, to actress Jill Baleon, he developed into an outstanding public reader of poetry. All told, in addition to the detective fiction (always more psychological and symbolic than violent) he produced twenty volumes of verse, four novels, anthologies, literary criticism, and an autobiography. His latest work, *The Whispering Roots* (1970), revealed the two characteristics of his verse from beginning to end. With deep Georgian roots, his central concern was for others, a continuing compassion which for one brief decade found poetic expression as political sympathy for the oppressed. It is of special coincidence for this study which links the Romantics, the thirties' poets, and the fifties' poets, that Day-Lewis died at the home of his friend, Kingsley Amis, one of the chief Angry Young Men of the fifties.

Stephen Harold Spender, whose chief poems of the proletarian decade were collected in *Ruins and Visions: Poems 1934–1942*, made a frank confession of his disillusionment with communism in an essay contributed to Richard Crossman's collection *The God That Failed* (1949). UNESCO counsellor in the Section of Letters, 1947, he became the co-editor of *Encounter*, 1953. Often lecturing in British and American universities, he occupied the Elliston Chair of Poetry, University of Cincinnati, 1953; he was Beckman Professor at the University of California, 1959, and visiting lecturer at Northwestern University, 1963. He delivered the Clark Lectures at Cambridge University, 1966, and was visiting professor at the University of Connecticut, 1969.

At the beginning a poet whose verse soared wildly or fell noncommittally flat, with a burden of feeling that exceeded its artistic expression, he remained a rhetorical writer floating on the clouds of his own adolescent emotions and the hero worship and millennial hopes of the Victorian era.

Lacking the wit of MacNeice and Auden, it has always been a Romantic lyrical impulse that has sustained his poetry and a touching idealism that engaged his audience. His most recent volumes of poetry are *Selected Poems* (1965) and *The Generous Days* (1971). His special concern for children and youth found continued expression in *The Year of the Young Rebels* (1969). The confessional aspect of his poetry and prose excelled in frank self-revelation, in deeds of imaginative and emotional charity, in a masochistic need to suffer and forgive—all stated with chronology-defying innocence.

In a previous full-length study of the art of Louis MacNeice, I have delineated at length his circular movement.[5] From *The Last Ditch* (1940), he climbed to scriptwriter and producer for the B.B.C. The verse plays *Christopher Columbus, The Dark Tower, Prisoners' Progress,* and *Traitors in Our Way* come out of this association. In 1942 a second marriage granted the poet a lyrical Spring and the vaudeville rhythms of Auden & Co. started to lose their hold. *Holes in the Sky: Poems 1944–1947* begins to show the new MacNeice as *Ten Burnt Offerings* (1952) and *Visitations* (1957) reveal him completely. Thematically the poet has returned to the great issues of life, love, death, and faith that concerned him in his juvenilia. A metaphysician rather than a moral philosopher on the order of Auden, the classical humanism that animated him as professor of Classics at Birmingham University 1930 and University of London 1936 returns in full measure during the last eleven years of his creativity. Stylistically the proletarian poet has wiped his pen of smokestacks, wars, and socialism, and dipping in a deeper well, penned long-flowing, ample-length poems on those topics of love and death that moved him the most.

It seems strange that the ideological development of a poet so arrogantly sure of his own judgments as Wystan Hugh Auden can be traced in terms of personal discipleships to Sigmund Freud, Georg Groddeck, Homer Lane, Karl Marx, Dante, Søren Kierkegaard, Jesus Christ, Horace, and Goethe. The first three writers supply diagnostic skills to analyze that sickness the poet observes in men (*Poems* [1928], *Paid on Both Sides* [1930], *The Orators* [1932], *The Dance of Death* [1933], *The Dog Beneath the Skin* [1935], and *The Ascent of F6* [1936]).

Auden's prescriptions for the human ailment quite naturally move to the body politic during his Marxist period (*Look, Stranger!* [1936], *Spain* [1937], *Letters from Iceland* [1937]). *On the Frontier* (1938), *Journey to a War* (1939), and *Another Time* (1940) might represent his "infernal" vision of the twin predicaments of man and society; 1940 being the date of his Christian conversion, *New Year Letter* (1941), *For the Time Being* (1944), and *The Age of Anxiety* (1947) arise from his discipleship to the Christian revelation, via the twisting Damascus road of that melancholy Dane, Kierkegaard.

As the insistent voice grows less strident because it is more sure and more urbane because it is less desperate, a newer and more elegant Horatian poetry is produced in *Nones* (1951), *The Shield of Achilles* (1955), and *About the House* (1965). The almost frightening versatility of the man, expressed in youth by metrical experiment and parody, in maturity finds Goethean expression in criticism—*The Dyer's Hand* (1962), and in libretti, written alone or in collaboration with Chester Kallman.

The verbal virtuosity of the elegant MacNeice has been exercised and the traditional lyricism of Day-Lewis has sung its last song. The hard-core intellectuality of Auden has produced its angular verse and of the soft-core emotionalism of Spender, the best that can be stated—there is more in store!

Notes

1 — C. Day-Lewis

1. Marvin Barrett, *The Years Between* (Boston and Toronto: Little, Brown and Company, 1962), p. 5.
2. Day-Lewis, *A Hope for Poetry*, p. 36.
3. Justin Maynard Replogle, "The Auden Group: The 1930s Poetry of W. H. Auden, C. Day Lewis, and Stephen Spender" (Ph.D. diss., Unversity of Wisconsin, 1956)., chapter 6: "Evolution of Social Thought."
4. C. Day-Lewis and L. A. G. Strong, eds., *A New Anthology of Modern Verse: 1920–1940* (London: Methuen, 1941), p. xxi.
5. David Daiches, *Poetry and the Modern World: A Study of Poetry in England Between 1900–1939* (Chicago: University of Chicago Press, 1940).
6. Raymond Tschumi, *Thought in Twentieth-Century English Poetry* (London: Routledge and Kegan Paul, 1951).
7. Translation by Peter Glare (the editor of the *New Oxford Classical Dictionary*).
8. *A Hope for Poetry*, p. 48; *Collected Poems of C. Day Lewis*, pp. 136–37.
9. Day-Lewis, *Starting Point*, p. 31.
10. Ibid., p. 285.
11. Ibid., p. 317.

2 — Stephen Spender

1. Spender, *World Within World* (Hamilton), p. 95; (Harcourt) p. 87.
2. Spender, *The New Realism*, p. 8.
3. Ibid., p. 12.

4. Ibid., p. 14.

5. Spender, *Trial of a Judge*, act 3: "The Large Scene."

6. Spender, *The Backward Son*, p. 100.

7. Spender, *The Still Centre*.

8. *World Within World* (Hamilton), pp. 136–37; (Harcourt), pp. 125–26.

9. Spender, *The Burning Cactus*, p. 104.

10. Ibid., p. 154.

11. *The Backward Son*, p. 51.

12. Spender, *The Destructive Element*, p. 11.

13. *World Within World* (Hamilton), p. 139; (Harcourt), p. 128.

14. Derek Stanford, *Stephen Spender, Louis MacNeice, C. Day Lewis: A Critical Essay* (Grand Rapids: Wm. B. Eerdmans, 1969), p. 17.

15. *World Within World* (Hamilton), p. 115; (Harcourt), p. 105.

16. Barrett, *The Years Between*, p. 100.

17. *World Within World* (Hamilton), p. 132; (Harcourt), p. 121.

18. The Destructive Element, p. 228.

19. Ibid., p. 232. Cf. Max Eastman, *Artists in Uniform: A Study of Literature and Bureaucratism* (New York: Alfred A. Knopf, 1934), Chapter 1.

20. *The Destructive Element*, p. 233.

21. *The Still Centre*.

22. *World Within World* (Hamilton), pp. 262–63; (Harcourt), pp. 238–39.

23. *The Burning Cactus*, p. 107.

24. *The Destructive Element*, p. 36.

25. Ibid., pp. 254–55.

26. *The New Realism*, pp. 20–21.

27. *World Within World* (Hamilton) p. 312; (Harcourt), p. 283.

28. *The Still Centre*.

29. Ibid.

30. Ibid.

31. Ibid.

32. Ibid.

33. *The Burning Cactus*, p. 124.

34. Ibid., p. 129.

35. Ibid., p. 132.

36. Ibid., p. 148.
37. *The Destructive Element*, pp. 59–60.
38. Ibid., p. 98.
39. Ibid., p. 200.
40. *World Within World* (Hamilton), p. 241; (Harcourt), p. 219.
41. Spender, *Forward from Liberalism*, pp. 201–2.
42. *World Within World* (Hamilton), p. 202; (Harcourt), p. 184.
43. Ibid. (Hamilton), pp. 290–91; (Harcourt), p. 264.
44. *The Burning Cactus*, p. 84.
45. Ibid., pp. 85–86.
46. Ibid., p. 86.
47. Ibid., p. 146.
48. *The Backward Son*, p. 20.
49. *World Within World* (Hamilton), p. 183; (Harcourt), p. 167.
50. Ibid. (Hamilton), p. 184; (Harcourt), p. 167.
51. Ibid. (Hamilton), p. 185; (Harcourt), p. 168.
52. Ibid.
53. *The Burning Cactus*, p. 73.
54. Ibid., p. 96.
55. Ibid., p. 104.
56. Ibid., p. 130.
57. Ibid., p. 150.
58. *The Backward Son*, p. 55.

3—Louis MacNeice

1. MacNeice, *Blind Fireworks*, Foreword.
2. Louis MacNeice, *Christopher Columbus: A Radio Play* (London: Faber and Faber, 1944).
3. *Times* (London), December 6, 1937, p. 18c.
4. *New York Times*, August 9, 1953, section 7, p. 7.
5. MacNeice, *Modern Poetry*, p. 189.
6. W. H. Auden and Louis MacNeice, *Letters from Iceland*, p. 20.
7. MacNeice, *I Crossed the Minch*, p. 3.
8. Ibid., p. 14.
9. Ibid., p. 11.
10. Ibid., pp. 124, 125, 127–28, 130, 136, 138.
11. Ibid., p. 159; MacNeice, *Collected Poems*, p. 97.
12. *I Crossed the Minch*, p. 245.

13. "When they are in model zoological gardens, the animals, even though separated from the climate of their habitat, are surrounded by comfort and attention. When they become accustomed to their situation, they prefer the peace and security of captivity to the freedom and terrors of wild life" (MacNeice, Zoo, p. 239).

14. Zoo.

15. *Modern Poetry*, p. 112.

16. Ibid., p. 176.

17. Ibid., pp. 32, 34.

18. Ibid., p. 198.

19. Louis MacNeice, "The Poet in England Today," *New Republic*, March 25, 1940, p. 4.

20. Julian Symons, "Louis MacNeice: The Artist as Everyman," *Poetry*, May 1940, p. 92.

21. Edmund Wilson, ed., *The Collected Essays of John Peale Bishop* (New York: Charles Scribner's Sons, 1948), pp. 310–11.

4—Wystan Hugh Auden

1. Spender, *World Within World* (Hamilton), p. 54; (Harcourt), p. 49.

2. Ibid.

3. Ibid. (Hamilton), pp. 54–55; (Harcourt), pp. 49–50.

4. Ibid. (Hamilton), p. 54; (Harcourt), p. 49.

5. Ibid.

6. Ibid. (Hamilton), p. 55; (Harcourt), p. 50.

7. Replogle, "The Auden Group," p. 32.

8. Ibid.

9. Auden, *The Orators*, p. 14.

10. John Lehmann, *The Whispering Gallery: Autobiography* (London and New York: Longmans, Green, 1955).

5—From Romantic Revolution to Welfare State

1. William Wordsworth, *The Prelude*, book 11.

2. George Gordon, Lord Byron, *Childe Harold's Pilgrimage*, canto 3, stanza 18.

3. Elton Smith and Esther Smith, *William Godwin*, English Authors Series (New York: Twayne Publishers, 1965).

4. John Osborne, *Look Back in Anger: A Play in Three Acts* (London: Faber and Faber, 1957).

5. Elton Smith, *Louis MacNeice*, English Authors Series (New York: Twayne Publishers, 1970).

Selected Bibliography

C. Day-Lewis

Beechen Vigil and Other Poems. London: Fortune Press, 1925.
Collected Poems of C. Day Lewis. London: Jonathan Cape with the Hogarth Press, 1954.
Country Comets. London: Martin Hopkinson, 1928.
From Feathers to Iron. London: Leonard and Virginia Woolf at the Hogarth Press, 1931.
A Hope for Poetry. Oxford: Basil Blackwell, 1934.
The Magnetic Mountain. London: Leonard and Virginia Woolf at the Hogarth Press, 1933.
Noah and the Waters. London: Leonard and Virginia Woolf at the Hogarth Press, 1936.
Overtures to Death and Other Poems. London: Jonathan Cape, 1938.
Revolution in Writing. London: Leonard and Virginia Woolf at the Hogarth Press, 1935.
Starting Point. London: Jonathan Cape, 1937; New York: Harper and Brothers, 1938.
A Time to Dance and Other Poems. London: Leonard and Virginia Woolf at the Hogarth Press, 1935.
Transitional Poem. London: Leonard and Virginia Woolf at the Hogarth Press, 1929.
Word Over All. London: Jonathan Cape, 1943.

Stephen Spender

The Backward Son: A Novel. London: Hogarth Press, 1940.
The Burning Cactus. London: Faber and Faber, 1936.
Collected Poems: 1928–1953. London: Faber and Faber, 1955.

The Destructive Element: A Study of Modern Writers and Beliefs. London: Jonathan Cape, 1935.

Forward from Liberalism. London: Victor Gollancz, 1937.

The New Realism: A Discussion. London: Hogarth Press, 1939.

Poems. London: Faber and Faber, 1933.

Poems for Spain. With John Lehmann. London: Leonard and Virginia Woolf at the Hogarth Press, 1939.

Returning to Vienna, 1947: Nine Sketches. New York: Banyan Press, 1947.

Selected Poems. London: Faber and Faber, 1940.

The Still Centre. London: Faber and Faber, 1939.

Trial of a Judge: A Tragedy in Five Acts. London: Faber and Faber, 1938.

Twenty Poems. Oxford: Basil Blackwell, 1930.

Vienna. London: Faber and Faber, 1934.

World Within World: Autobiography. London: Hamish Hamilton, 1951; New York: Harcourt, Brace and Company, 1951.

Louis MacNeice

Autumn Journal. London: Faber and Faber, 1939.

Blind Fireworks. London: Victor Gollancz, 1929.

The Collected Poems of Louis MacNeice. Edited by E. R. Dodds. New York: Oxford University Press, 1967.

The Earth Compels: Poems. London: Faber and Faber, 1938.

I Crossed the Minch. London: Longmans, Green, 1938.

The Last Ditch. Dublin: Cuala Press, 1940.

Letters from Iceland. With W. H. Auden. London: Faber and Faber, 1937.

Modern Poetry: A Personal Essay. London: Oxford University Press, 1938.

Out of the Picture: A Play in Two Acts. New York: Harcourt, Brace and Company, 1938.

Oxford Poetry, 1929. Edited by Louis MacNeice and Stephen Spender. New York: D. Appleton, 1929.

Poems. London: Faber and Faber, September 1935.

"The Poet in England Today." *New Republic*, March 25, 1940, p. 412.

"Poetry Today," *The Arts Today*. Edited by Geoffrey Grigson. London: John Lane, 1935, pp. 25–67.

Roundabout Way. Louis Malone, Pseud. London and New York: Putnam, 1932.

Selected Poems. London: Faber and Faber, 1940.

"Subject in Modern Poetry," *Essays and Studies* 22. Oxford: At the Clarendon Press, 1937, pp. 144–58.

Zoo. London: Michael Joseph, 1938.

Wystan Hugh Auden

Another Time. London: Faber and Faber, 1940; New York: Random House, 1940.

The Ascent of F6: A Tragedy in Two Acts. With Christopher Isherwood. London: Faber and Faber, 1936.

The Collected Poetry of W. H. Auden. New York: Random House, 1945.

The Dance of Death. London: Faber and Faber, 1933.

The Dog Beneath the Skin, or Where Is Francis? With Christopher Isherwood. London: Faber and Faber, 1935.

In Time of War. London: Faber and Faber, 1939.

Journey to a War. With Christopher Isherwood. London: Faber and Faber, 1939.

Letters from Iceland. With Louis MacNeice. New York: Random House, 1937.

Look, Stranger! London: Faber and Faber, 1936. American version: *On This Island.* New York: Random House, 1937.

A Melodrama in Three Acts: On the Frontier. London: Faber and Faber, 1938.

New Year Letter. London: Faber and Faber, 1941.

The Orators: An English Study. London: Faber and Faber, 1932.

Poems. London: Faber and Faber, 1930.

Spain. London: Faber and Faber, 1937.

Index